TRIUMPH
The Legend

TRIUMPH
The Legend

Mac McDiarmid

PARRAGON

Page 1: Craig Vetter's radical Triumph X-75 Hurricane design. Page 2: One of the best of the 'Hinckley' Triumphs, the ultra-versatile 900 Sprint. Page 3: Into the 21st century: the latest T509 and its T595 stablemate have launched Triumph to new heights of performance and technology. Page 5: The 900 Tiger 'monster trailie' has been a major hit in European markets.

Figures and data in this book are quoted in metric measurements first, with the Imperial equivalents noted in brackets.

This is a Parragon Book

© Parragon 1997

Parragon
Units 13-17, Avonbridge Trading Estate,
Atlantic Road, Avonmouth,
Bristol BS11 9QD

Designed, produced and packaged by
Stonecastle Graphics Ltd.,
Old Chapel Studio, Plain Road, Marden,
Tonbridge, Kent TN12 9LS, United Kingdom

Edited by Philip de Ste. Croix

ISBN 0-75252-080-6

Printed in Italy

Photographic credits:
All photographs by **Mac McDiarmid** except:

EMAP (Classic Bike/Classic Motorcycle):
pages 1, 7 *(left)*, 10, 11, 12, 13, 14, 15 *(top)* 16, 17 *(top)*, 18, 23, 27 *(right)*, 28, 29, 31 *(top)*, 32, 33, 34, 38, 39, 42, 43, 44 *(right)*, 45 *(left)*, 46 *(left)*, 47 *(top)*, 48 *(left)*, 52 *(left)*, 54, 55, 56, 57, 58 *(top)*, 78, 79.

Triumph Motorcycles: page 3, 7 *(top)*, 9 *(right)*, 63 *(top)*, 72 *(top)*.

Triumph Motorcycles America: page 48 *(right)*.

Special thanks are also due to the **National Motorcycle Museum**, Birmingham, UK, for their cheerful assistance with many of the photographs in this volume.

Contents

Introduction	6
The Early Years	8
To The First World War	10
The Twenties	14
Triumph Ricardo	18
The Thirties	20
Turner's Tigers	24
Triumph Speed Twin	26
The Second World War	28
Post-War Rebuilding	30
Triumph 650 6T Thunderbird	36
Record-Breaking Triumphs	38
The Sixties	40
The Triumph Scene	46
Triumph T120 Bonneville	50
The Threat From Japan	52
Triumph Trident 750	54

Co-operation and Collapse	58
Rebirth: Bloor Triumph	60
Into the Nineties	62
Triumph Daytona 900 and 1200	64
Triumph Daytona Super III	66
Triumph Trophy 900 and 1200	67
Triumph Sprint 900	68
Triumph Speed Triple	70
Triumph Trident	72
Triumph Tiger 900	73
The New Look	74
The Dream Factory	76
Competition	78
Index	80

Introduction

Triumph Motorcycles are many things, not the least of which is miraculous. When John Bloor's new Triumph factory began producing a range of new, modern machines in late 1990, the world at large was slow to take notice, but something truly wonderful had happened. Here, in the heart of England was a brand-new, ultra-modern manufacturing plant, paid for with British money and producing a range of products with an altogether British name. Even the best-informed financial journalist would be hard-pressed to cite a comparable example over the past 20 years. Nothing of this scale has been created except with foreign capital and, more often than not, an overseas name. Yet this one was totally home-grown.

More surprising still, this Phoenix was actually making motorcycles – and good ones, at that. Since selling its first new machine in early 1991, New Triumph has gone from strength to strength. Sales have risen dramatically year-on year. Production efficiency has improved at a similar rate. Quality – already high at the outset – has improved to industry-high standards. A second, even bigger factory is scheduled to come on-stream early in the

Left: 56 years separates the 1939 Tiger 100 from the 1995 Thunderbird (above), but both are unmistakably Triumph.

21st century. And, on the eve of 1997, a second generation of new Triumphs threatens to compete with the very best in terms of handling and performance.

Yet surprisingly for a company which can lay claim to a longer history of motorcycle production than any other (although not quite continuous), John Bloor's energetic project has made a point of *not* trading on the past. The attitude has always been: 'We compete on our merits, not on the rosy glow of nostalgia'. This, as much as the company's space-age technology, has been the key to their modern success.

And yet, there is much in Triumph's long history of which they can be proud. In the early years of the century, Triumph did as much as anyone to change motorcycles from rich men's unreliable playthings into a practical and enjoyable means of transport (characteristics the military were also glad of through two World Wars). In the Twenties they became a powerful force in British industry which also gave rise to the range of motor cars which, until quite recently, also bore the same Triumph name.

But perhaps Triumph's biggest claim to fame is the creation of the archetypal British motorcycle, and through it the archetypal biker, world-wide. In 1937 a young Triumph engineer by the name of Edward Turner produced a 500cc twin cylinder design which was to be imitated by many of his rivals for the next four decades. The immortal Speed Twin, as it was known, became the benchmark by which other motorcycles were judged. It led directly to other classic Triumph from

Below left: Two, three, or four? Triumph legend 'café racer' built by equally legendary race-tuner Les Williams employed a 750cc T140 Bonneville twin engine. Below: Adventurer is a 900cc triple custom cruiser. Left: Lavishly equipped Trophy tourer used 1200cc four-cylinder power.

the Tiger 100 to the legendary Bonneville, and even (with the addition of another cylinder) to the mournful racing wail of the all-conquering triples of the early Seventies.

Although the blame lay with men rather than machinery, the Speed Twin and its descendants also led to the death of the British motorcycle industry. As well as charting the Triumph company's many successes from 1902 to the present, Triumph – The Legend also traces the decline and ultimate decay of what was once the greatest motorcycle industry in the world. This period is littered with tales of inaction, short-term greed and sheer incompetence which give the lie to the notion that Japan – or anywhere else – was actually responsible.

But we can all take heart, as this book is delighted to, that this decline was not the end of the story. The modern Triumph company is a stirring example to all who believe that manufacturing still has a future in Britain.

7

The Early Years

LIKE THAT other archetypically 'English' motorcycle manufacturer, Velocette, Triumph was in fact founded by a German. Siegfried Bettman was aged 20 when he arrived in Britain from Nuremburg in 1883. Two years later this wealthy, well-educated young man had founded a company to sell bicycles overseas. Within a year he had discarded the family name in favour of one with a more patriotic ring, and Triumph came into being. A year later still the formal title 'The Triumph Cycle Company' was adopted. He didn't know it at the time, but adding the word 'motor' would create a legend which has set the pulse racing for most of the intervening 112 years.

Initially Bettmann simply bought in and re-badged bicycles made for him by William Andrews, but when he was joined by an engineer, Mauritz Schulte (also from Nuremburg, where 23 years later Triumph would found a subsidiary factory), he was able to establish a small factory to manufacture his own wares. Suitable premises were located at a former ribbon-weaving shop in Much Park Street, Coventry, then the centre of the British cycle trade. Capital came from the partners themselves, from two Coventry businessmen and, later, from the nearby Dunlop tyre company.

In the same year that Bettmann founded his company, another German, Gottlieb Daimler, installed the first internal combustion engine in a self-propelled bicycle. In 1894 Hildebrande and Wolfmüller began manufacture of the first production motorcycle. These early attempts were impractical, primitive, unreliable and slow (2.5 horsepower from 1530cc), but the strange new technology was rapidly gathering pace.

As the 20th century dawned, eager young men throughout the industrial world were experimenting with this new breed of internal combustion engine. Nowhere was this more true than in the English Midlands, the epicentre of light engineering and a hotbed of innovation. Most such experiments would lead nowhere, but the sheer energy of these enterprises infused Schulte with ideas of his own. (He had in fact contemplated building Hildebrande and Wolfmüllers under licence). In 1902 he produced Triumph's first powered two-wheeler – a modified bicycle with a 1 3/4 horsepower Belgian Minerva engine strapped to the frame. Schulte continued to experiment with other proprietary powerplants (including the wonderfully-named Fafnir, and a 293cc JAP which can be seen in the National Motor Museum). But there was really only one way Schulte could meet his own exacting standards. Three years later Triumph built their first engine.

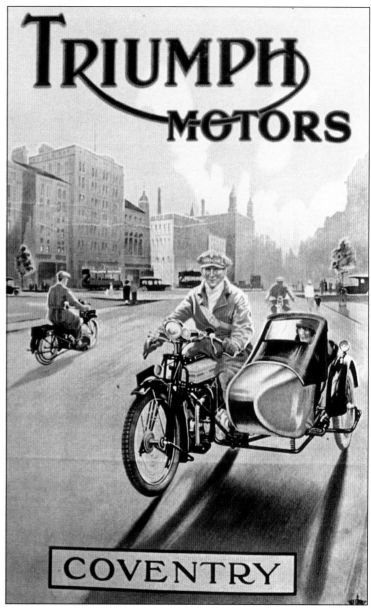

It is no coincidence that the word 'engine' comes from the same Latin root as 'ingenious', and the meticulous Schulte spent long hours refining his creation. As well as the structure of the engine itself, the great debate at the time was where best to place it. There were proponents of all manner of peculiar positions (one of which – over the front wheel – survived to the present day with the French VeloSolex). Triumph first favoured a position ahead of the bicycle's pedals, but it was not long before it migrated 'amidships' to the location familiar today. And with that, the first 'proper' Triumph was born.

Left: Triumph's first model (from 1902) can be seen in the national Motorcycle Museum near Birmingham's NEC.

Above: The first 'Triumph' engine was a Belgian Minerva side-valve, but within three years the new company progressed to producing its own powerplants.

Right: Halcyon days from an early publicity poster: empty roads, sunny skies, and an Edwardian gentleman travelling the Triumph way.

To The First World War

SCHULTE WAS, by all accounts, a cautious man, a meticulous designer and tester who demanded the highest levels of craftsmanship in his creations. Since even the best motorcycles of these early years were unreliable contraptions, his instincts quickly earned Triumph a priceless reputation for quality and dependability. It should be born in mind that at the time literally hundreds of tiny workshops were making motorcycles, and only marques of quality could expect even fleeting survival.

The first Triumph engine was a side-valve single of 363cc (78 x 76mm), with an ingenious method of actuating the valves from cutaways in the timing gears. It was also reputedly the first engine with ball main bearings, capable of generating three horsepower at 1500rpm. Drive was taken by leather belt to the rear wheel. In 1907 it grew to 453cc, then by degrees to 550cc, a capacity it retained well into the Twenties.

Below: Triumph's first in-house engine was a surprisingly sophisticated 363cc single, although the machine's frame was soon found wanting.

Nor was Triumph's effort confined to engine development. The fork blades were stoutly reinforced, whilst the frame, unusually, boasted twin front downtubes – although the design was to prove fatally flawed. Ignition was by trembler coil, although a magneto could be supplied for £5 more than the basic price of £45.

The next major development was the famous Triumph sprung fork which was to endure well into the Twenties. In 1906, the formidable motorcycle journalist Ixion conducted a lengthy test of a prototype 1907 machine. It was a disaster. Not only did the engine lose power, but the frame broke. However Triumph's reputation was restored when the reconditioned engine was quickly rebuilt into a single-downtube frame, on which Ixion clocked up a prodigious 2058km (1279 miles) in six days. In the same year Frank Hulbert scored Triumph's first major competition success when he won the Dashwood hill climb on a prototype which was to become the 1907 453cc '3 ½hp' model.

Triumph produced some 500 machines during 1906, a figure they doubled on moving into new premises at Priory Street, Coventry, a year later. 1907, of course, is best remembered for the first running of the Isle of Man motorcycle TT (the cars had one in 1906). Although Matchless won the single cylinder class, Jack Marshall's Triumph finished a worthy second. A year later he went one better, averaging 65km/h (40.40mph). However, once their reputation was established Triumph became much less competition-minded: it would be another 59 years before they chalked up their second TT success.

Nonetheless, machine improvements followed steadily. 1908 brought a carburettor of Triumph's own manufacture, engine controls moved to the handlebars (obvious now, but less so at the time), and the factory's first attempt at variable gearing. This required the rider to stop to move the drive belt between pulleys, but was better than having to push up hills. Capacity had also risen, a 2mm (0.078in) boring job now giving 476cc (84 x 86mm).

Right: W. Creyton pictured on one of eight 499cc Triumphs which completed the 1910 TT. Below: By 1908 the Triumph rocking fork was acknowledged as one of the best. The carburettor, too, was of Triumph manufacture.

By 1910 production was running at over 3000 machines per year. There was a further capacity increase – to the 499cc of the previous year's TT machines. But it is best remembered as a year for feats of startling endurance. Although victory again eluded Triumph at the TT, every one of the eight 3 1/2hp Triumphs competing scored a solid finish.

The feat was not lost on Triumph's marketing people, for it later gave rise to the sporting 'Tourist Trophy' Roadster – possibly the first 'race replica'. For good measure Albert Catt clocked up no less than 3038km (1888 miles) in six days on single speeder – yet was disappointed not to have surpassed his target of 3219km (2000 miles).

Below: One of 30,000 machines supplied to the military during the First World War, this Model H formed the army's communications backbone. When the shrapnel flew, Triumph's growing reputation for reliability offered far more than mere sales hype. Right: The modest little 225cc two-stroke LW 'Baby' was one of Triumph's first lightweight successes.

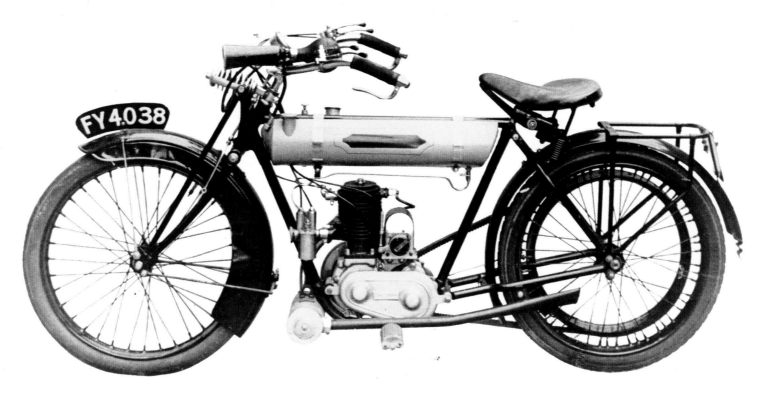

Had Catt ridden a 1911 model, he might have made it. The year brought the first Triumph with a clutch. Although this was located in the rear hub, it was a welcome novelty as it allowed the rider simply to drive off, rather than having to run alongside before leaping precariously onto the saddle. By 1913 the basic big single was offered in a variety of options: with and without clutch; with variable gear (belt drive); or with the new three-speed hub gear.

Despite their later association with twins and then triples, Triumph's formative years were all about singles, although Schulte had begun toying with the idea of a twin-cylinder machine as early as 1910. His initial prototype employed a proprietary French engine. This later gave way in 1913 to Triumph's own twin, a 600cc side-valve with horizontally-split crankcases (which wouldn't reappear until the late '50s). Regrettably the First World War intervened, and the project lapsed. The other departure from the norm was a range of two-stroke singles, beginning in 1913 with the two-speed 225cc Triumph LW Junior designed by Charles Hathaway. Nicknamed the 'Baby', this was to last until 1925, latterly as a 250.

In the year in which war broke out, Triumph's flagship model was the 'four horsepower' Type A Roadster, now of 550cc (85 x 97mm). Not the least of its attributes was the new Bosch high tension magneto, a superb device which single-handedly transformed the reliability of any motorcycle so endowed. A similar machine, the indomitable Model H, was to form the backbone of Britain's two-wheeled war effort. No less than 30,000 were supplied to the military. With the three-speed Sturmey Archer gearbox, chain primary drive, a transmission shock absorber, 'semi-automatic' carb and chain-driven magneto, they served their country – and Triumph – well.

Inevitably the return to peace after 1918 was a time of uncertainty for most sectors of manufacturing industry. For Triumph a difficult readjustment was further marred when the unthinkable happened: Schulte left the company after falling out with Bettmann. It would take something special to replace the man who had so brilliantly guided Triumph Motorcycles through their formative years.

The Twenties

THE TWENTIES was to prove a decade of ironies for the growing Triumph concern. The cause of Schulte's departure in 1919 had been his wish – vigorously opposed by Bettmann – to see the company diversify into the manufacture of motor cars. And yet this was precisely the course which would be pursued by his successor.

The Twenties was also the decade in which Triumph introduced two of their most innovative models, the Ricardo and the LS. Yet neither prospered – one, because Triumph seemed to lose their enthusiasm, the other because the public never showed any. Instead, the model which sold in

colossal numbers was arguably one of the worst Triumphs ever made, an exercise in cost-and-corner-cutting known as the Model P. Nonetheless, it is for the legendary 'Riccy' that the period is best remembered.

Schulte's successor as general manager was Colonel Claude Holbrook, who had become known to Bettmann through his motorcycle procurement role for the War Office during

the First World War. Where Schulte had failed, Holbrook was successful in closing down Triumph's bicycle production in favour of entering the rapidly growing car market. The company's first four-wheeler, introduced in 1923, was a 1393cc open tourer designed by Harry Ricardo.

Ricardo, of course, was also the creator of the sensational four-valve two-wheeler described on pages 18-19. Triumph's boldest model, however, would be a great deal cheaper. Prior to 1925 Triumph's commercial progress had been based on

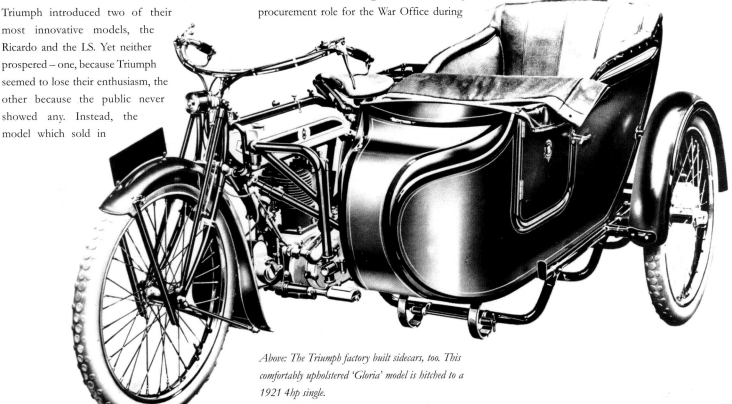

Above: The Triumph factory built sidecars, too. This comfortably upholstered 'Gloria' model is hitched to a 1921 4hp single.

Schulte's instinctive dictum of a modest stream of technical developments and a commitment to quality of manufacture. 1920 had brought the 4hp Type SD, with three-speed, Triumph-made gearbox, multiplate clutch and, finally, all-chain transmission with an oil bath primary chaincase. The 'SD' stood for spring drive, a transmission shock absorber necessitated by the chain drive. It was a necessary selling point as chain-driven machines had previously been associated with harshness compared to the more forgiving qualities of belts. The SD's engine was otherwise derived from the old 550.

Other improvements followed year-on-year: rim-type brakes finally gave way to internally-

Above: The clean lines of the 346cc Model LS incorporated an advanced unit construction engine and 'automatic' oil pump, but performance was not startling and it did not sell well. Right: By now, the Baby's leather belt drive was also showing its age.

expanding drums; electric lights and horn were offered (albeit as optional extras). Most novel of all was the Type LS of 1923, a very advanced 350cc side-valve three-speeder with gear primary drive and an engine-driven oil pump where previously the rider had had to apply the oil pressure by hand. Unaccountably, the LS failed to inspire the buying public and was soon withdrawn.

Despite the decade's popular epithet of the 'Roaring Twenties', its early years brought more of a whimper to much of manufacturing industry. The post-war recession had brought rampant inflation and difficult times. Triumph's response was startling, the cheapest 500cc motorcycle ever offered for sale. At less than £43, the 1925 Model P substantially undercut everything else on the market, driving several rival companies out of business almost overnight. Predictably, the 494cc side-valve single was in huge demand. Less predictably, it was a mess, full of design flaws and short-cuts which gravely affected reliability: for Triumph had not only lost Schulte, in pursuit of competitiveness they had lost sight of his perfectionism. By the time improvements came in late 1925 with the Mk2, 20,000 had been built, but Triumph's reputation had been sorely tarnished.

By this time Triumph had become a huge operation. The factory now occupied some 46,450m² (500,000 square feet), on which 3000 employees could produce as many as 1000 Model Ps alone each week. Sidecars were also made in-house in large numbers, either coachbuilt 'luxury' chairs or commercial boxes. An increasing proportion of overall production now went abroad. Exporting had become the key to success, with Triumph catalogues produced in ten languages, including (ironically, perhaps) Japanese.

Despite their commercial success, during the mid-Twenties Triumph seemed less than clear as to where their future lay. In 1927 a new but far less ambitious middleweight single, the 277cc side-valve Model W, was introduced to replace the unsuccessful LS. But in other respects the company appeared to favour a future manufacturing cars. For 1928 the motorcycle range was slashed from eight to a mere four models, as the factory concentrated on its new four-wheeler, the Super Seven.

Below: The notorious Model P was so cheap it proved a disaster for Triumph's competitors, and so nasty it was almost calamitous for Triumph itself.

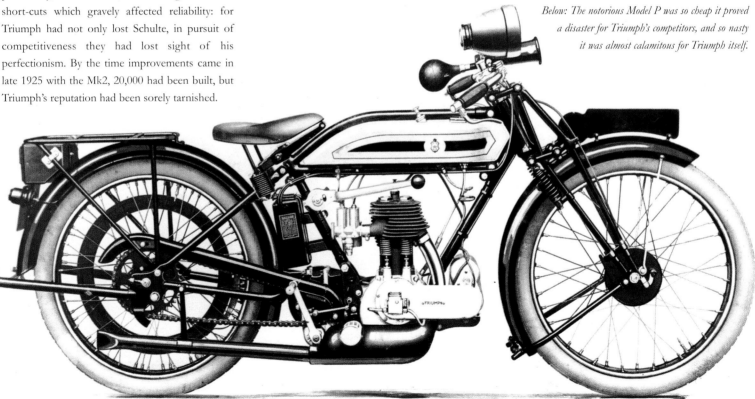

16

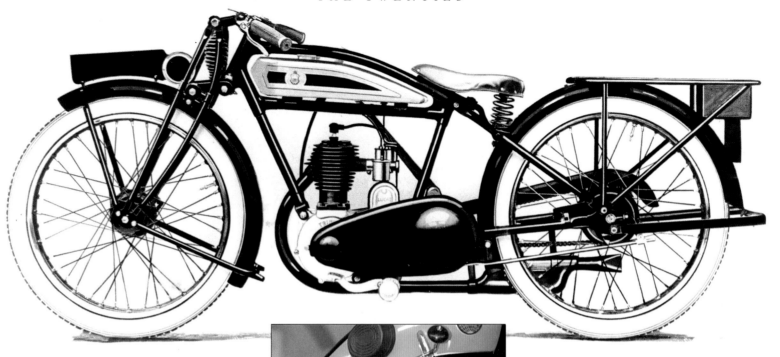

1929, however, brought a return to reason – at least as far as two-wheeled fans were concerned. Again there were eight models in the Triumph range. Despite – or, perhaps, because of – the Ricardo's influence, side-valvers continued to dominate, including the CSD (548cc), NSD (548cc) CN (498cc) and NL (494cc). In addition there was the new 350cc CO, with enclosed overhead-valve gear and a dry sump pressurized oil system. The flagship model remained the 498cc ST, derived from the same Victor Horsman's TT model which had ousted the Ricardo.

Despite debacles such as the first Model P, and the sorry neglect of the Ricardo's potential, the

Above: The 277cc Model W replaced the 'Baby' as the bargain-basement Triumph model, although now it was a side-valver rather than a two-stroke. At this time Triumph became besotted by car production, but soon returned to their senses. Left: At the other end of the scale lay this striking 500cc ohv CTT of 1930.

Twenties had seen Triumph grow to become a giant of the British motorcycle scene. It was also the decade in which motorcycles came of age, beginning to look less like motorized bicycles and more like the machines of today. Hard times, however, were just around the corner as the decade came to a close.

Triumph Ricardo

THROUGHOUT most of their history, Triumph had been relatively slow to adopt new technology, preferring to leave that sort of thing to others while they soldiered on with proven ways of doing things. All that changed with the 'Ricardo' four-valver with which Triumph contested the 1921 TT.

Harry Ricardo – later to become Sir Harry – was arguably the outstanding genius of the early years of automotive engineering. Marked as a brilliant applied scientist from his undergraduate days at Cambridge, it was Ricardo who first developed a true understanding of the breathing and combustion processes of the four-stroke engine. Not surprisingly, it was to Ricardo & Co. Ltd. that Triumph turned when they decided to move with the times.

When Triumph announced their first, Ricardo-designed, overhead-valve Triumph in 1921, the entire industry was agog. Although basically comprising a Ricardo top-end mated to a Model H bottom-end and chassis, the TT model had the most exotic specification. Its cylinder head not only featured a pent-roof combustion chamber, but no less than four valves controlled the gas flow. The cylinder, containing a light alloy piston, was machined from a solid billet of carbon steel. Bench testing revealed a healthy peak power output of 20bhp at 4600rpm.

For the 1921 TT Triumph fielded two squads, one riding the old side-valve racer, the other composed of three 'Riccy' models. The underdeveloped newcomer fared poorly, with only

Below: Although not produced in great numbers, Harry Ricardo's four-valver is regarded as one of the masterpieces of 1920s' motorcycle engineering.

18

Left and above: The Model R featured Druid forks, hand gearchange and bicycle-type stirrup brakes at the front.

one machine finishing the race, in 16th place (a side-valver came fifth). Nonetheless, improvements followed and in 1922 a Ricardo with shorter stroke, larger valves and Druid forks placed second at the TT. The machine was ridden by the brilliant Walter

SPECIFICATION	RICARDO
ENGINE	air-cooled, ohv, 4-valve, single
POWER	20bhp @ 4600rpm
TRANSMISSION	3-speed
TOP SPEED	135km/h (84mph)

Brandish who two years later would break his leg in crashing a similar machine at the corner now named after him. Even in November 1921, however, the four-valver would show its potential, with Major F.B. Halford breaking the world 500cc one hour record at 123.49km/h (76.74mph), and the British flying mile record at 135.04km/h (83.91mph).

Had Triumph persevered, the Riccy might have become a dominant force in racing. But, for whatever reasons, the factory saw its interests as lying elsewhere and concentrated its efforts instead on the Type TT two-valver developed and raced at

Surrey's famous banked Brooklands circuit by Victor Horsman. This was to become Triumph's stock competition machine until the early Thirties, also forming the basis of the flagship ST sports model.

Nonetheless, in 1922 the racing Riccy – or something very like it – was offered for public sale. The four-valve Model R had a barrel of iron rather than steel and Druid forks rather then the Triumph springers which had so alarmed its riders on the Isle of Man. The cost? – £120. After a reign that showed more potential than triumph, the Model R was discontinued in 1927.

The Thirties

THE WALL Street crash of 1929 plunged global manufacturing industry into an enduring slump which rang the death knell for innumerable motorcycle companies. Triumph's large and fairly efficient operation initially fared better than many, partly thanks to a range of unprepossessing two-strokes of 150 and 175cc.

One model even committed the folly of using a humble 98cc Villiers engine although, to save face, Triumph marketed these under the brand name 'Gloria'.

But despite drastic cost-cutting, Triumph's major creditors, notably Lloyds Bank, insisted on even more rigorous measures. Bettmann was forced

Below: The two-stroke 'Gloria' was one of Triumph's answers to the world-wide sales slump of the Thirties' Depression.

Right: Although the Speed Twin is far better known, Val Page's 650cc 6/1 was Triumph's first four-stroke vertical twin.

Left: The handsome 500cc 5/5 of 1936, a top-of-the-range sporting single. One year later, under Edward Turner's inspired direction, it would become the revered Tiger 90.

under a 'spare' trading name hanging over from 1906: Triumph Engineering Co. Ltd. With the name went the manufacturing rights to the motorcycles, the Priory Street factory and much of its plant – for a princely £5000. Sangster shrewdly (if temporarily, as it turned out) re-appointed Bettmann as chairman, which went down well with trade and public alike.

As well as considerable business acumen, Sangster had two other ace cards. At Ariel, he had the good sense, or good fortune, to install as successive chief designers two men who would rank amongst the elite. One was Val Page, who had subsequently joined Triumph in 1932; the other was Edward Turner, designer of the Ariel Square Four, who had joined Ariel in 1928.

Despite the difficulty of launching major new models during the depression, Triumph's design department had not been idle prior to Sangster's arrival. As well as evolving a new range of single cylinder models, both side- and overhead-valve, Page had created Triumph's (and Britain's) first four-stroke vertical twin, the 122km/h (76mph) 650cc 6/1, first offered for sale in 1933.

By now the specifications across the range were reaching more modern standards: the transmission was now four speed (with foot change a £1 optional extra), the large diameter brakes worked well. A Lucas Magdyno supplied the ignition and electrical systems, and Amal provided the carburettor.

to stand down as managing director and in 1935 the unthinkable became policy: motorcycle production was to cease, with the Priory Street works to be sold off. Car production would continue at Foleshill Road, Coventry.

At this point salvation arrived in the form of J.Y. 'Jack' Sangster, who had breathed new life into the beleaguered Ariel company earlier in the slump. On 22nd January 1936 Triumph cars and motorcycles became separate entities, the latter

Just like the modern Triumph factory at Hinckley, Page's design philosophy favoured a modular approach, with 250, 350 and 500cc models sharing almost the same chassis. Top of the singles range was the 5/5, with the substantially similar 5/2 being a 'cooking' variant. (The /5 tag denoted a tuned engine.) Most prized of all was the 5/10, essentially a stripped-down racer with high compression pistons, special flywheels, con-rods, hand-ported cylinder heads and lightened valvegear. The 5/10 was capable of close to 161km/h (100mph) and, after early teething troubles, performed well in competition. At the opposite end of the market, Triumph's two-stroke tiddlers were replaced by more sophisticated machines, the X05/1 and X05/5, powered by a new 147cc four-stroke 'sloper' single.

Although overshadowed by Turner's subsequent twin, the 6/1 was a formidable machine, having covered 805km (500 miles) in as many minutes at Brooklands in 1933 – with sidecar attached. Turner himself described it as 'extremely well engineered'. Like the later twin, it featured a 360 degree crankshaft, but with plain big ends and a single camshaft to the rear of the cylinders, rather than the twin cams of Turner's design. One advanced feature was the practice of bolting the four-speed gearbox rigidly to a flat on the rear of the crankcase, an arrangement which permitted a helical gear primary drive rather than the adjustable chain which would lumber the Speed Twin and its

Right: 5/5 engine in detail. The stroke-5 of the designation indicated a tuned engine. Stroke-10 signified an even more potent variant intended for competition use.

successors. This meant that the engine ran 'backwards', although there was no harm in that. This was essentially the range which Turner inherited when he took over from Page as Triumph's chief designer in 1936. Page went on to make his mark by helping create first BSA's A7, the superb Gold Star, and then the highly original Leader and Arrow ranges of Ariel two-strokes.

EDWARD TURNER

If Bettman and Schulte were Triumph's prime movers, then Edward Turner was the man who most consolidated their vision. His engineering career began in an anonymous machine shop in Dulwich, South London. It was here that he conceived his first masterpiece, the engine which was to become the Ariel Square Four.

Turner's original concept was far from the 1000cc leviathan that the four would later become. The compact 497cc four featured all-aluminium construction, horizontally-split crankcases and a single overhead camshaft. It was this design that in 1928 persuaded Jack Sangster to give him a chance at Ariel, where he initially worked under Page. His first project was a technically advanced 350cc cammy single. Although this never reached production, the square four did. The prototype, housed in a 500 'sloper' frame and weighing only 150kg (330lb), became the sensation of the 1930 Olympia motor cycle show.

Left: Edward Turner, the man most closely associated with Triumph's glory years, and particularly the trend-setting Speed Twin. Although an engineer by training, Turner had a special knack for spotting the style and image sought by the public, which made his creations more desirable than all the rest. His first act at Triumph was to drastically re-style the existing range.

But it was when Sangster took him to Triumph in 1936 that Turner's true brilliance shone.

Almost overnight he turned a capable but essentially mundane range of motorcycles into a beacon of British motorcycling. When he added the immortal Speed Twin a year later, his reputation was assured. With Charles Parker at his side to control the finances, he was to guide Triumph through their greatest years, even finding time to design the Daimler V-8 car engine. And when well into retirement, it was to Turner that Triumph turned in 1967 when the threat from Japan was finally taken seriously.

Turner the man was by all accounts a determined and impatient person who 'knew what he wanted . . . nobody got in his way.' Yet paradoxically, despite his unparalleled reputation as a designer of motorcycles, he was inept at many day-to-day matters; and as a mechanic he was 'hopeless'. He retired as Triumph chairman in 1964 and died in 1973.

His gift was less that of a pure engineer than of a designer of evocative machines. Possibly unique for his time, he had a rare sense not only of what would work, but of what could also fire the public imagination. And in putting the glamour into motorcycles – Triumph motorcycles – he did more than any other man to inspire the Legend that his company was to become.

23

Turner's Tigers

TURNER'S FIRST major act was to axe Page's rather staid 650cc twin and revamp the existing range of 250, 350 and 500cc overhead-valve singles. Lashings of chromium plate and a bold silver livery gave the trio a litheness they had hitherto lacked. More power and vibrant new names completed the change of identity: now the dowdy ring of models L2/1, 3/2 and 5/5 gave way to the roar of Tigers – Tiger 70, 80 and 90 respectively. In each case the number was their notional top speed. Slightly humbler versions of each, the 2H, 3H and 5H, were also introduced, with only the 3S (350cc) and 6S (600cc) remaining of the old side-valve fleet. With the slump ending, Triumph was ready for good times ahead.

Turner's enduring creation, however, was entirely his own. In July 1937 the 500cc Speed Twin was first unveiled. This startling vertical twin caused a flurry at least as intense as the Model P of a dozen years earlier, but for altogether more positive reasons. For the next four decades, offspring of this single model would be the definitive British motorcycle, imitated by many but never surpassed.

Below and opposite: The racy-looking 500cc Tiger 90 (this is a 1937 model) was the flagship model of Turner's range of re-styled singles, although the smaller Tigers were no less striking in appearance.

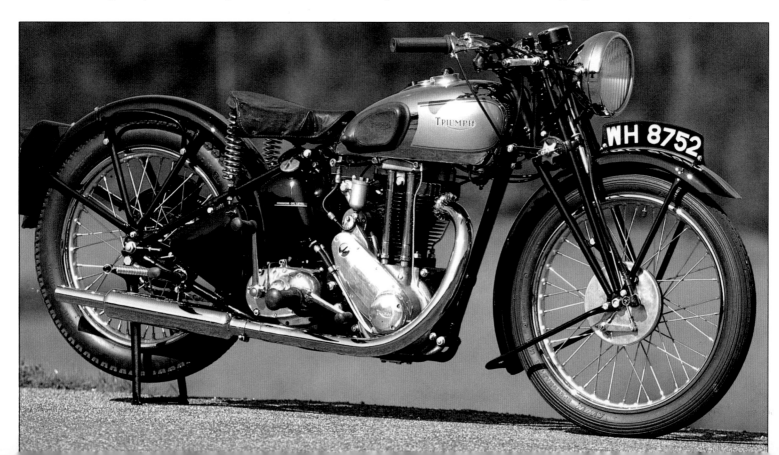

SPECIFICATION	TIGER 70	TIGER 80	TIGER 90
ENGINE	249cc ohv single	349cc ohv single	497cc ohv single
POWER	16bhp @ 5800rpm	20bhp @ 5700rpm	28bhp @ 5700rpm
TRANSMISSION	4-speed	4-speed	4-speed
WEIGHT	141kg (310lb)	145kg (320lb)	166kg (365lb)
TOP SPEED	106km/h (66mph)	121km/h (75mph)	141km/h (88mph)

All three came equipped with four-speed gearboxes, enclosed valvegear, dry sump lubrication, Amal carbs and 6v Lucas Magdyno. The Tiger 90 also boasted a polished con rod and flywheels and hand-finished ports. When new, in 1938, the Tiger 70 cost £55. The 80 cost £61 and the 90 cost £70. For an extra £7, specially equipped competition models of all three were available, with extra ground clearance, q.d. lighting and other refinements.

Triumph Speed Twin

IF A single model can lay claim to being uniquely Triumph – indeed the quintessential British motorcycle – the Speed Twin unveiled in 1937 is it. The 500cc twin was Edward Turner's first all-new engine design since arriving at Norton from Ariel. It looked good, went superbly and captured the public imagination in a way which Val Page's 6/1 twin quite

failed to do. More than any other machine it lifted Triumph's fortunes out of the slump of the mid-Thirties, and set them on the road to success for a further four decades.

Priced at £77 15s 0d when launched, the twin scored with a conservative public partly by looking much like a single when viewed from the side. With

a bore and stroke of 63 x 80mm (the same as the existing L2/1 250cc single), it displaced 498cc. Transmission was by gear primary drive to a wet, multiplate clutch and four-speed gearbox.

The combustion chambers were hemispherical, each featuring two valves. Twin camshafts, fore and aft of the cylinders, were driven by spur gears from the crankshaft. The pushrods moved in tubes located in slots in the cylinder fins, operating the valves by means of short, stiff rockers. The crankshaft was of pressed-up construction with a

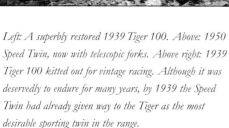

Left: A superbly restored 1939 Tiger 100. Above: 1950 Speed Twin, now with telescopic forks. Above right: 1939 Tiger 100 kitted out for vintage racing. Although it was deservedly to endure for many years, by 1939 the Speed Twin had already given way to the Tiger as the most desirable sporting twin in the range.

SPECIFICATION	SPEED TWIN
ENGINE	498cc ohv parallel twin
POWER	27bhp @ 6500rpm
TRANSMISSION	4-speed
FUEL TANK	13.6 litres (3 gallons)
TOP SPEED	145km/h (90mph)

substantial flywheel bolted on centrally in such a way as to minimize the flexing to which the relatively long, unsupported cranks of two-bearing twins are prone.

Turner housed his engine in what was essentially a Tiger 90 chassis and running gear but, despite its twin-cylinder engine, the twin weighed no more than the single. Peak power was 27bhp, good for a top speed of around 132km/h (82mph), but what was more remarkable was the effortless manner with which the twin reached this speed. Sadly the outbreak of war prevented the debut of a 350cc sister model, scheduled for release in 1940.

Having brought out the 'ultimate', Turner

followed it up with an even better version in 1939, a practice he was to continue for decades. This was the 158km/h (98mph) Tiger 100, a sporting version of the Speed Twin. The Tiger boasted a larger carburettor, forged high compression slipper pistons, polished internals and a hand-ported cylinder head, raising peak power to 33bhp and top speed to a mercurial 158km/h (98mph). Inevitably sports twins found themselves used for competition – at least when early crank problems were resolved and Bert Hopwood had modified the geometry to reduce the machine's notorious speed wobble. Indeed the ends of the silencers were readily removed for precisely this purpose.

The Second World War

WHEN WAR broke out in September 1939, Triumph immediately directed their energies towards the war effort, with their exciting new models taking a back seat until the end of hostilities. In total Triumph supplied almost 50,000 bikes to the forces, beginning with the requisitioning of civilian models, then hastily militarized versions of their redoubtable side-valvers, the 3SW and 5SW.

Prior to the war, Triumph had begun work on a prototype military workhorse, the 3TW, which was to compete with others for ministry contracts. Turner conceived an unexpectedly sophisticated machine, an ohv 347cc twin with unit construction (not to appear on civilian Triumphs for almost 20 more years) and the first motorcycle alternator electrical system. After evaluation, the 3TW received the nod from the government, and production of the first batch of 50 machines began.

They were never to reach service. On the night of 14th November 1940, a 400 bomber blitz struck Coventry. The Triumph factory, and the adjacent cathedral, were flattened. Miraculously the entire Triumph night shift was able to retreat to the shelters and survive a raid which accounted for over 500 civilian deaths. For the 3TW, however, it was the end of the line.

Triumphs were never again built on the old Priory Road site. Production was hurriedly moved to a temporary factory in Warwick, where production resumed in June 1941. The other problem was precisely what to build. Enter the 3HW, based on the pre-war ohv 343cc 3H single and far easier to make than the 3TW twin. Meanwhile a brand new factory was built alongside the main Coventry to Birmingham road at Meriden (reputedly the centre of England). This became operational in the Spring of 1942, building 3HW and 500cc vertical twin engines for use in portable generators. One, the lightweight AAPP (Airborne Auxiliary Power Plant) charged the batteries of RAF bombers in flight – small revenge for the shattered factory of 1940. This lightweight design, with silicone-aluminium head and barrel, had obvious competition potential when peace returned, and Ernie Lyons used a Tiger 100 so equipped to win the 1946 Manx Grand Prix. The same construction was later applied to the Grand Prix and TR5 Trophy models.

Another lasting legacy of war was the TRW. In 1942, much to Sangster's disgust, Edward Turner had briefly defected to Triumph's foremost competitor, BSA, where he worked on a military side-valve twin. Sangster charged his new chief designer, Bert Hopwood, with developing a rival. After some clever bluffing, this effectively put paid to the BSA challenge, although the war was over before the resulting model 5/3W stumbled into production. This later became the TRW which, despite its side-valve engine, was in other respects a clever design.

The 500cc twin incorporated several of the advanced features of Turner's 3TW and shared many chassis parts with the TR5 Trophy. Over 7500 were built, with many continuing in service, mainly overseas, well into the Sixties. Hopwood himself, in the merry-go-round that was the British motorcycle industry, went on to design Norton's answer to the Triumph Speed Twin.

Left: TW military machine: production was blitzed into oblivion in November 1940, forcing Triumph to a new home.

Above: 1940 was Britain's darkest hour. Here, members of the British Expeditionary Force enjoy a well-earned break after evacuation from the beaches of Dunkirk. The machine with such an epic story to tell? A civilian model Triumph 350cc 3S.

Post-War Rebuilding

MERIDEN'S RESPONSE to the reopening of civilian markets was as bold as Turner's Tigers had been a decade before. The new battle cry was twins, twins, and more twins. For the first time in the company's history, not a solitary single featured in the Triumph line-up.

Contemporary brochures had it otherwise. You could read about a 350cc single in 1946. You could also read about a brand new twin, the Tiger 85. But you couldn't buy either one of them. The factory was so stretched trying to meet the public's voracious appetite for the top-of-the-range twins, that the humbler models disappeared by default. And the old side-valve models, at least for civilian markets, were consigned to history.

Yet the post-war 5T Speed Twin and Tiger 100 were essentially 1939 models, although some improvements had been made. There were new telescopic front forks, revised electrical systems and the four-gallon (18.2-litre) tanks originally scheduled for 1940 had Hitler not decreed otherwise. (Thanks to 'pool' petrol, they were also slower then pre-war.) The period also brought the first Triumph with rear

Below: A Speed Twin in the colour – Amaranth Red – which became almost as well-known as the bike. By the time this model was built – 1940 – most of Triumph's competitors had developed Speed Twin clones.

suspension – of sorts. In 1946 Lyons' MGP-winning twin had employed Triumph's first attempt at rear suspension, in which the springs were contained within an oversize rear wheel hub. The 'Sprung Hub' which later reached the roadsters was essentially a stop-gap measure until resources allowed the creation of a new swinging-arm frame.

As well as the big twins, a 350cc twin belatedly also hit the showrooms in 1946. Loosely based on the aborted 3TW, the 20bhp 3T De Luxe had been scheduled for launch in September 1939, the very week in which war broke out. But by far the most momentous new model was unveiled in 1949: the legendary 6T Thunderbird. The T'bird is dealt with in detail in the next chapter, but suffice it to say that a Speed Twin with added poke was precisely what the public desired. At a mere £10 more than the Speed Twin, it soon became Triumph's most desirable model.

With demand comfortably outstripping supply, Triumph had little interest in competition, which they evidently regarded as an expensive distraction. When reluctantly persuaded to enter a trio of 500 twins in the 1948 Senior TT, the result was retirement for each, a failure that did nothing to change long-term policy.

The lack of an official factory race team was not to imply that the company was blind to performance-orientated publicity – it was simply that they preferred to stage manage their own. Such was the case with Thunderbird in 1950, when a trio of the new 650s hurtled round the French Montlhéry track for 805km (500 miles) at an average 145km/h (90mph), before being ridden back to Meriden.

Above: A 1953 army TRW twin, a dependable old soldier developed from Bert Hopwood's wartime 5/3W, incorporated many clever features from Turner's pre-war 3TW.

Below: The rigid rear end gives this Speed Twin clean classic lines but does nothing for ride quality. Rear suspension was just around the corner.

31

Triumph also continued to produce models suitable for trials, scrambling and clubmans road racing but now they, too, were twins. First came a 350. Then in the 1948 ISDT (International Six Day Trial), the sole British team prize was won by a squad of special Speed Twins prepared by Harry Vale and ridden by Allan Jefferies (father of current TT star, Nick), Jim Alves and Bert Gaymer. Triumph were quick to exploit their success. Within a year the TR5 Trophy went on sale. Lighter and shorter than the ISDT machines, with 25bhp from an AAPP top-end and two-into-one exhaust, this quickly became one of the most sought-after models. After 1951, die-cast aluminium cylinder barrels replaced the earlier sand-cast versions. Their elegantly close-finned design became a characteristic Triumph feature. A 650cc version, the TR6, was added in 1956. Although notionally related to the later, baser, Trophy Trail and Adventurer models, these were real thoroughbred machines.

Nor were hot roadsters neglected, particularly in the growing Stateside market. Throughout the Fifties a comprehensive factory tuning kit was available for the Tiger 100, and from 1957 to 1970 the most sought-after Triumph part in the USA was TriCor's huge tuning goodies catalogue. As well as special T100Rs, there was the very rare TR5R of 1956, a competition hybrid incorporating the best parts from TR5, TR6 and T100. It was a worthy successor to the immortal Grand Prix model discontinued in 1950.

Left: Even military Triumphs could do this. Alasdair Graham of the Royal Signals puts a TRW through its paces.

The USA, a market Turner had long coveted, was also obsessed by cee-cees. In 1951 Triumph founded an American subsidiary, the Triumph Corporation of America (TriCor). This, and a separate West Coast importer, oversaw a rise in sales volume from £680,000 in 1951 to £7.5 million (24,700 machines) in 1967. At its peak, the USA accounted for over two-thirds of Triumph production.

America was also the scene of one of the more legendary exploits in Triumph lore. In 1956 Johnny Allen took a 650cc Triumph streamliner to a world best speed of 344km/h (214mph) on Utah's Bonneville salt flats. Although this sensational feat was not accepted as a record by the FIM, to the public that three-digit figure was all that mattered.

The Fifties was also a decade of momentous business matters for Triumph. Triumph's entry into the US market had terrified Harley-Davidson, the sole surviving domestic manufacturer. Compared to Meriden's fast and agile roadsters, the American V-twins were crude, cumbersome and overpriced. Milwaukee's first response was to attempt to prevent their dealers from stocking the foreign hardware. Then, alleging that British machines were being 'dumped' at artificial prices, they applied to Washington for an import surcharge to be levied. It took Congress little time to see the myth in this, and they just as promptly charged Harley with restrictive trade practices. Ironically for both parties, the resulting judgment was to pave the way for the Japanese invasion two decades later.

Below: A 1953 5T Speed Twin. Note closely-finned die-cast cylinders and sprung-hub rear suspension, a half-way house to full swinging-fork rear ends.

Affairs were no quieter at home. In 1951 Jack Sangster, who had sold Ariel to the mighty BSA group in 1939, sold Triumph to the same bidder. The price was £2.5 million, of which Edward Turner's holding earned him a tidy ten per cent for his retirement. In practice this had little immediate effect on the motorcycling public, for Triumph and BSA designs would go substantially their separate ways until the late Sixties.

Five years later, however, the tables were turned. After a bitter boardroom struggle, Sir

Below: The elegant lines of a 1953 T110 Thunderbird mask its thunderous performance potential, although it could not quite reach the '110' of its title.

Above: The same T'bird and its kid brother, a 500cc Speed Twin. Initially, the two models were almost identical save for cylinder capacity.

Bernard Docker was ousted as chairman of the BSA group. And who but Jack Sangster should be appointed to take the helm? Practically his first act as chairman was to appoint Edward Turner as chief executive of BSA's automotive division, which included Daimler cars as well as Triumph, BSA and Ariel motorcycles. Sangster retired in 1960.

Despite such backroom turmoil, the latter half of the Fifties was a golden period at Meriden, whose model range was vigorously updated. Just as the Tiger 100 had been an uprated sporting Speed Twin in 1939, so the Tiger 110 was the logical next step up from the basic Thunderbird. In 1952 a new unit construction lightweight arrived. The 149cc Terrier featured a new overhead-valve inclined engine (visually not unlike the X05/5), offering 8bhp at 6000rpm. In 1954 this was to become the remarkable 199cc Tiger Cub on which so many trials careers began. Although the Terrier featured a plunger rear end, this was yet another halfway house on the road to full swinging-arm suspension, which was established throughout the range by 1956.

A year later still, the first unit construction engine finally arrived, with the gearbox and crankcases sharing a common casting. This far superior construction first appeared with the 349cc/20bhp Model 21 and T100A, and would reach the rest of the twins by the early Sixties. In 1959, substantially the same machine, but now displacing 490cc, became the latest version of the Speed Twin. The engine was now undersquare (69 x 65.5mm), the shorter stroke allowing higher revs and a peak power of 27bhp. Then, as the decade drew to a close, Turner unveiled his definitive sporting twin. Tiger 110 begat Bonneville T120 and the ton-up era began.

Below: The 500cc TR5 (this is a 1954 model with die-cast cylinder barrels) grew out of Triumph's ISDT success. Later it was enlarged to become the potent 650cc TR6.

Triumph 650 6T Thunderbird

AMERICA HAS always loved ultimates, and the 650cc Thunderbird was no exception. Indeed the decision to enlarge the Speed Twin's 500cc engine to 650cc was taken largely to propel Triumph's assault on the US market. First unveiled in 1949, this is probably the motorcycle best known to the post-war generation. For this was the machine ridden so defiantly by Marlon Brando in the 1952 film *The Wild One*: 'What are you rebelling against, Johnny?' 'Whaddya got?'.

What you got was a light, agile motorcycle offering genuine 161km/h (100mph) performance, an experience hitherto reserved exclusively for racing motorcycles. The T'bird wasn't quite the fastest machine around – that distinction lay with Vincent – but as a package it redefined public expectations of what two wheels could deliver. It was simply a great motorcycle: the Z1 or Fireblade of its time.

In essence the early T'bird was identical to the contemporary Speed Twin, itself substantially a pre-war design, other than the extra 150cc and a change of colour. The air-cooled engine is separate from the gearbox, linked by an enclosed single-row chain. Valve actuation is by push rods from gear-driven paired camshafts fore and aft of the crankcase mouth.

Rear suspension was by Triumph's ubiquitous Sprung Hub, for the rear swinging fork had barely arrived. Oil-damped telescopic forks of Triumph design had first replaced girder suspension on the

Above: Although spurred chiefly by US market ambitions, the growth to 650cc was no less well received at home. Note full swing-arm rear suspension.

SPECIFICATION	650 6T THUNDERBIRD
ENGINE	649cc air-cooled, ohv, parallel twin
POWER	34bhp @ 6300rpm
TRANSMISSION	4-speed
WHEELBASE	1397mm (55in)
WEIGHT	180kg (397lb)
TOP SPEED	166km/h (103mph)

'Saint' became the standard two-wheeler for forces around the UK and abroad, although its characteristic white livery didn't actually appear until the mid-Sixties. Later TR6P police bikes were also known as Saints.

Yet just as the Tiger 100 had evolved as the high-performance version of the Speed Twin, so the need was clear for an even hotter version of the T'bird. The result was first the Tiger 110 of 1954, then the legendary Bonneville. Development of the T'bird continued, adding more power, swing-arm rear suspension and, in 1963, unit construction. The latest tribute came in 1994 when born-again Triumph announced a 900cc model with the same evocative name.

1946 Speed Twin. Overall, the Thunderbird was a lighter machine than most in its class, with vivid acceleration provided by a free-revving engine.

For Triumph, additional costs of the first affordable 'ton-up' machine were modest, and even in the shops the difference between 500 and 650cc was a mere £10, the T'bird costing just £194 when introduced. Not surprisingly, BSA, Norton and Royal Enfield were quick to join the big twin bandwagon.

One of the best-remembered versions of the T'bird was the 6T police model. Thanks to its combination of speed and manoeuvrability, the

Above: The T'bird engine offered genuine ton-up performance.

37

Record-Breaking Triumphs

As WELL as lending their name to Triumph's most famous model, Utah's Bonneville Salt Flats are the home of two- and four-wheeled record-breaking. With the nearest hospital 160 kilometres (100 miles) from the sun-blasted desert, it is also a home for heroes. In late Summer each year (weather permitting), the Flats host 'Speed Week', when aspiring record-breakers and crackpots make the trek to the desert sanctuary. Needless to say, Triumph has played a notable part in the story.

Bonneville's advantage for breaking records is the sheer vastness of the dry lake bed, allowing huge distances for bikes to run up to speed, hit the timing lights, and decelerate. But the sheer remoteness is a problem for high-tech teams. The nearest civilization is the tiny town of Wendover, which lies at an elevation of 1372 metres (4500 feet) – not conducive to maximum power.

Triumph first entered the Bonneville record books in 1956 when Johnny Allen took a cigar-shaped 'streamliner' powered by a 650cc Triumph twin engine to 344km/h (214mph). Although the 'record' was one-way and thus not recognized by motorcyling's international body, the FIM, it captured the imagination of the motorcycling public. Three years later, Triumph's hottest new model borrowed the Bonneville name.

In September 1962 Bill Johnson set the record straight, piloting another twin-cylinder streamliner

Below: Triumph personnel admire the fastest cigar in the world, Johnny Allen's 'record breaking' 650cc streamliner. The device would put the immortal 'Bonneville' name into Triumph brochures.

at an average of 361.40km/h (224.57mph) over the two-way measured mile. The record-breaking machine subsequently attracted huge crowds when displayed at the Earl's Court motorcycle show. The 180kg (397lb) projectile was over 5 metres (16ft 3in) long, with a wheelbase of 240cm (94.5in). The engine and transmission were behind the rider, who lay on his back in a device little higher than a man's knees. The engine ran on methanol at a compression ratio of 11:1. Despite its top speed, there was just a single puny drum brake on the rear wheel.

In 1966 Bob Leppan flew the Triumph flag even higher into the stratosphere, posting 395.24km/h (245.6mph) with his twin-engined streamliner, Gyronaut X-1. Again, this was not a world record as the FIM capacity limit was one litre, and this aerodynamic monster displaced almost 1300cc.

Leppan and his engineer Joe Bruflodt were big Triumph dealers in the 'Motor City' of Detroit. They later built a three-engined version whose suspension collapsed at around 434km/h (270mph), seriously injuring Leppan. Even without this catastrophe, he had mixed feelings about the record-breaking business: 'It's treacherous, the bike's weaving . . . following every little rut and tyre track in the salt. There's nothing to get you out of trouble . . . there's just you and the salt and this amazing sensation of speed.

Nor was record-breaking confined to the big stuff. In 1959 Bill Martin took a 199cc Tiger Cub-powered streamliner to an astonishing two-way average of 225.01km/h (139.82mph), with a best one-way of almost 241km/h (150mph).

In recent times jet-propelled vehicles have taken the outright speed records, but there are still

Above: Johnny Allen on his way to 344km/h (214mph). Although no return run was possible and Triumph was not officially credited with a new record, Allen and Triumph will forever be associated with this feat and with the vast baking salt flats of Utah. In 1962 Bill Johnson set the record straight.

men who prefer to wrestle with conventional projectiles with driven wheels. One of these, Ed Mabry, is still writing Triumph's Bonneville story. His 295kg (650lb) 'real motorcycle' houses two Trident three-cylinder engines, built by the same Jack Wilson who assembled Johnny Allen's famous machine. In 1991 Mabry's rider, Jon Minonno, took it to a two-way mean of 356.49km/h (221.52mph). A year later he clocked a staggering 403.34km/h (250.63mph), but was unable to repeat this on a second run.

The Sixties

THE SIXTIES was the Bonneville decade. Triumph's first twin-carb roadster had first appeared in 1959, but the initial styling job was curiously staid, with the Speed Twin's nacelled headlamp and distinctly unsporting mudguards carried over. But by 1960, the stylists had got it right. Anyone with £285 to spare could now have this genuine 'ton-plus' machine, perhaps the fastest standard production motorcycle in the world.

The glorious 'Bonnie' was, of course, a hopped-up Tiger 110, with a light alloy splayed-port cylinder head, higher compression ratio, twin Amal carbs without air cleaners and the omission of the automatic 'Slickshift' clutch found on cooking models. It was aimed principally at the increasingly important US market, which in 1960 also demanded – and got – a special twin-carb, Bonneville-engined Trophy, the TR7A. (The 'A' denoted a pre-unit street bike, competition models being suffixed 'B'. The equivalents after 1960 were 'R' and 'C'.) Surprisingly, sales took some time to get going in the USA, although the T120 was a huge and instant hit on this side of The Pond. Many regard the early Bonnie as Triumph's best post-war model.

Backing up Triumph's mouth-watering specifications were glowing test reports and a series of notable performance successes. The first came in 1962 at Bonneville – where else? – when Bill Johnson finally rectified Johnny Allen's omission in setting an official speed record of 361.40km/h (224.57mph) with a 650cc streamliner.

Then, in 1966, Triumph at last claimed their first Daytona road race victory. Following Buddy Elmore's success on a Tiger 100C – average speed 155.5km/h (96.6mph) – in 1966, Meriden unveiled a celebratory model, the twin-carb 500cc T100R Daytona, a tuned version of the T100A which had been completely redesigned for 1959. This in turn led to a sister model, the single-carb T100C 'street scrambler'. Both lasted until '72. In 1967 and again in 1968, Gary Nixon took the prized AMA Number One plate for Triumph.

Elsewhere in the range, the original Trophy series was discontinued in 1960, to be replaced a year later by the TR6S/S (for Street Scrambler), then the TR6SR and competition SC. These were very much US-flavoured devices, for the standard TR6 Trophy was very much more common on the home market. Essentially a single-carb Bonnie, this gave 40bhp @ 6500rpm. Although less comfortable on dirt than their predecessors, derivatives of this and the 500cc TR5 enjoyed considerable success in off-road competition. Both versions were practically unrivalled in the most gruelling off-road events such as the International Six Days Trial or American long-distance enduros.

1961 brought a new Tiger 110, which became an enduring and hugely popular roadster powered by a single-carb engine similar to the TR6. A year later the 6T Thunderbird was comprehensively revamped, now featuring unit construction, a two-into-one exhaust and full-width hubs.

40

The Sixties was also the decade of the remarkable little 199cc Tiger Cub. Although code-named as the T20, the Cub was capable of a good deal more than 32km/h (20mph) – indeed this was the machine on which Joey Dunlop's mercurial road racing career began. The Cub's agility and its punchy 10bhp engine brought it considerable trials success. In 1961 an extra £9 could buy the 14.5bhp T20 S/L sports model.

Sadly, with Japan about to muscle in on the small capacity scene, the T20 was the last truly successful lightweight that Meriden was to make. Ironically, in 1966 Suzuki had released their own T20, the massively successful Super Six, a six-speed, two-stroke twin capable of over 145km/h (90mph). Indeed the BSA Group's increasingly desperate efforts to create a credible replacement for the Cub and for BSA's comparable two-stoke Bantam would be partly responsible for the catastrophe that was to occur. For as the Sixties neared its conclusion, nothing radically new was in the pipeline. Even the triples (see pages 56-7), for all their brief glory, were makeshifts harking back to Edward Turner's design of over three decades before.

For if the Sixties was Meriden's most successful decade in the modern era, it was also the period during which things began to go badly wrong. 1967 brought Triumph's best-ever sales figures in the American market. Yet at the following winter's AGM, Eric Turner was to describe the BSA Group's figures overall as 'disappointing'. He, and the rest of the board, appeared to be aware that drastic measures were necessary, and that the Group's future could not long depend on an elderly twin and a stop-gap twin-and-a-half.

The Rocket-3/Trident 750 had been a joint venture, the first showroom model on which the collective efforts of BSA and Triumph had been brought to bear. But at around the time of the 'disappointing' sales figures, a more far-reaching joint venture had been set in motion by Eric Turner, who had taken over from Sangster as chairman. This was nothing less than the design and creation of 'probably the most comprehensive range of new models ever undertaken at one time.'

The identity of this 'comprehensive range', if ever it gained one, is an enigma. All the world at large ever saw was a 350cc twin, the Bandit, and its BSA equivalent, the Fury. What became of the rest, if they ever existed, is a mystery.

The 350, however, was an exciting machine – potentially. Designed by two eminently capable men in Bert Hopwood and Doug Hele, it was unveiled to the press and trade in the autumn of 1970. Its parallel twin engine featured twin overhead camshafts, producing 34bhp at 9000rpm, good for over 177km/h (110mph). The engine was a dry sump design, with vertically-split crankcases and five speeds, and an electric start version would be available. The price would be £380.

Below: Don Morley puts the remarkable Trials Cub through its paces. Right: Despite its tiny engine, the Cub showed the superiority of lightness and agility in this most technically demanding of all bike sports.

44

Above: Period leather, but the 59 Club, like Triumph, is still going strong. Right: Triumph Tina scooter. The coffee was far hotter stuff!

Brochures were printed, promises were made and in the spring of 1971 the world was waiting. Then . . . nothing. Initially the company stalled for time, blaming component suppliers, strikes, shortages of labour, and any other convenient scapegoat. Eventually an independent investigation revealed the sorry truth: production was utterly chaotic; under pressure to rush the new models into the shops there had been insufficient development time; component supplies – indeed the whole situation – were a shambles. The group had to perform a public and very embarrassing U-turn.

TRIUMPH SCOOTERS

The Sixties, of course, was also the scooter decade, and Triumph strived to get in on the act. A Turner-designed scooter, the Tigress, had first appeared in 1958. Available with either a 175 or 250cc ohv four-stroke engine, it was followed by the 100cc two-stroke Tina in 1962. Although the Tina featured quite advanced features – including automatic transmission – it proved unreliable. A much improved 'T10' version followed in 1965, but the Meriden scooters lacked the cachet of their Italian rivals and never really caught on. It also seems that many Triumph dealers were happier selling 'real' bikes to 'real' bikers.

Worse still, the failure to sell a single machine had huge financial implications (a situation made worse because when production ground to a halt, no-one had told BSA's swanky new computer to stop ordering parts). The debacle helped the company's overdraft to soar to over £22 million, way beyond that permitted, or prudent. The BSA Group's bankers were getting hot flushes and very cold feet. It simply couldn't go on like this. And it wouldn't.

Above: This chap wouldn't be seen dead on a scooter, even a Triumph. Left: Unfortunately, neither would almost anyone else. The Tigress was another expensive flop, but worse was to come.

The Triumph Scene

MOTORCYCLES may be made of metal, but the best of them also have soul. Owners don't simply use their bikes the way people might use a car or a fridge, they fall in love with them. And it's natural when people have such a fervent interest, that they club together to share their passion. This has been going on almost since the motorcycle was invented more than 110 years ago, and it's going on still.

Triumphs have soul, that's for sure. Triumph owners know that their bikes are the best. This is true even when the cussed thing has stranded you at midnight in pouring rain, but then love, as they say, is forever blind.

The high-point of the Triumph scene was also the high-point of Triumph itself, the heydays of the Fifties and Sixties, when every red-blooded youngster aspired to a Bonneville twin. Some, as newspapers were eager to point out, were the sort of bikers no respectable parent would want their daughter to bring home. Many others were tarred with the same brush: all bikers are rockers and all rockers go to Margate, beat up old ladies and fight mods. It wasn't true, of course, but much of the mud stuck.

But bikes, Triumph as much as any, did say 'rebellion'. They said 'this is our scene and our way of having fun, and you boring old folk aren't invited'. If it was galling to be typecast as a hooligan just because you happened to ride a Daytona, maybe there was also something rather attractive about being revered for some delinquent act you didn't even need bother commit.

Whether sipping tea at North London's Ace Cafe or cracking the ton on the blast down the A23 to Brighton, a Triumph twin made you a member of a very special club.

These were the people your mother warned you about if you grew up in the late Fifties and Sixties: Rockers. The fondly-remembered 'Ace Caff' on London's North Circular Road became a hallowed meeting point for a generation of ton-up kids. The name lives on in ventures such as Triumph twin specialists Ace Classics (below) in South-east London. Contemporary newspaper headlines would have you believe all Sixties' bikers were Attilla the Hun on two wheels, but most were simply youngsters having innocent fun. Besides, as all bikers know, the Mods were really to blame!

Above: You don't have to be a film star to enjoy a classic Triumph. This enthusiast is riding a 1979 US specification T140 D Bonneville. Right: Bad-boy Lee Marvin poses next to a Triumph twin during a break in filming.

You were also in very good company. Youth icons like James Dean also rode bikes. And didn't Marlon Brando himself ride a Thunderbird so rebelliously in the *The Wild One*? And Lee Marvin? And what else did Steve McQueen choose to blow off the Germans in *The Great Escape* but a Triumph twin? (How it got behind enemy lines is anyone's guess.) In 1958 even Buddy Holly's Crickets bought Triumphs: a 6T Thunderbird and a TR6A Trophy. Evidently they had wanted Harleys, until the salesman treated them 'like a bunch of bums'.

The hardware, too, was important. Sometimes a standard machine wasn't enough: custom paint, extra 'goodies', special tuning parts, all were eagerly gobbled up and bolted on. For a few even this wasn't enough. If a Triumph twin had a fault it was that it didn't have a Norton chassis. So, following racer Dave Degens' example, hundreds of owners bolted hot Triumph engines into Norton frames and the Triton was born.

Even today there's a buoyant Triumph scene, with classic Meriden twins still the favoured wheels

Below: The evocative qualities of Triumph twins continue to attract a dedicated market. This Hyde Harrier dates from the early Nineties.

of many who prefer 'real' motorcycling to the more antiseptic attractions of modern machines. There's even a small but a thriving industry providing 'new' cafe racers in the Sixties mould, lead by seasoned Meriden hands such as Norman Hyde.

Taking a leaf out of Harley's book, Hinckley, too, is endeavouring to create an image around its own thoroughly modern products. For Triumph not only sells motorcycles, but accessories, designer clothing and bric-à-brac – everything the well-heeled Triumph man might desire.

49

Triumph T120 Bonneville

THE IMMORTAL 'Bonnie' was Triumph's first twin-carb engine since the legendary Grand Prix model. The name, of course, came from the famous Bonneville Salt Flats in Utah, where in 1956 Johnny Allen's streamlined T110 Triumph had clocked the sensational speed of 344km/h (214mph). The roadster wasn't quite that quick, but at just 178kg (393lb) and with 46bhp at 6500rpm (12 more than the original Thunderbird) it was 'the fastest production motorcycle in the world'. In 1960 a new one cost less than £285.

Described as 'perhaps the fastest point-to-point roadster produced in Britain today' by a contemporary road test, the T120 was *the* machine to have amongst 'ton-up' kids of the day. As many as 1000 per week were built, most destined for the giant US market. Reliability was good, particularly after some early lubrication and wear problems were resolved.

From the start the Bonnie enjoyed the much stronger one-piece crankshaft introduced in 1959, but other improvements followed year-on-year: twin downtube frame in 1960; unit construction in 1963; 12-volt electrics one year later. Perhaps most important of all was the arrival of Doug Hele at

Right and far right: Although few bikers could aspire to owning a Thruxton Bonneville such as this 1965 example, a small industry emerged to satisfy the fantasy. Clip-on handlebars, 'bacon-slicer' brake coolers and racing seats became a common sight on Britain's roads.

Triumph in 1962. The former Norton man was later to find fame as the inspiration behind the success of the 750cc three-cylinder racers, but his first job at Meriden was to improve the geometry and front suspension of Triumph's premier twin.

In 1961 an even more special version, the 188km/h (117mph) T120R, was introduced. But of all the many thousands of T120s produced,

undoubtedly the ultimate was the Thruxton Bonneville production racer. Only 58 of these very special 650 in-unit twins were built: 52 in 1965; six in 1966. In addition, a further six pre-unit examples were built before '65. The first outing of the example pictured was the 1965 Barcelona 24-hour race, from which it retired with a blown engine. Although essentially similar in appearance to a standard 'Bonnie' the Thruxton boasted many internal differences. The chassis enjoyed special racing forks, a steeper head angle, racing seat, handlebars and foot controls. In 1966 a Thruxton

Bonneville cost some £365, £65 more than a 'cooking' Bonneville; but only if you could get one. In full racing trim it could easily exceed 201km/h (125mph).

In 1968, and not before time, the Bonnie received the twin leading-shoe front brake developed for the new triples. There was a new, oil-bearing frame and in 1972 a 52bhp 750cc version, the T140, was added. But scarcely had a five-speeder arrived in 1973 than the Triumph/BSA group went bankrupt. The Meriden workers cooperative eventually took over production of the twins, including the £1149 limited edition 'Silver Jubilee' T140V. The last Meriden Bonneville was built as the cooperative collapsed in 1983.

SPECIFICATION	T120 BONNEVILLE (1960)
ENGINE	649cc air-cooled parallel twin
POWER	46bhp @ 6500rpm (later 51bhp @ 7100rpm)
TRANSMISSION	4-speed (later 120V: 5-speed)
WHEELBASE	1416mm (55.75in)
WEIGHT	179kg (395lb)
TOP SPEED	177km/h (110mph)

Left: Bonneville: possibly the most evocative name in motorcycling. Looks good, too.

The Threat From Japan

IN 1954 Edward Turner had visited Japan, taking keen notice of the emerging Japanese motorcycle industry. (Honda's first model had appeared in 1948, Yamaha's arrived in the year of Turner's visit.) The experience clearly had a considerable impact, for on his return he made a typically blunt observation to his chauffeur, Frank Griffiths: 'Do you know, my lad, if we don't pull our fingers out there won't be anybody making motorcycles in this country in 25 years time.' For once the great man was wrong. To all intents and purposes the British motorcycle industry died in 1983 – four years later than predicted.

And yet, if the writing was so clearly on the wall so long before the event, how was it allowed to happen? Like many great empires before it, the British motorcycle industry grew complacent, increasingly took its customers for granted, and became dismissive of competition from overseas. A culture of caution had arisen. Finance took precedence over engineering so, like much of UK industry, investment was low, with long-term

Left and above: Technically advanced but woefully underdeveloped, the Bandit (and similar BSA Fury) almost single-handedly brought BSA/Triumph to its knees.

planning sacrificed to short-term profits. The emphasis was on appeasing shareholders and an over-cautious board far more than on producing desirable products.

Although BSA's design centre at Umberslade Hall was almost space-age in its technology, it wasn't necessarily very switched on. (Group employees christened it 'Mecca' because there they could 'mecca balls-up of anything'). BSA's Small Heath factory was sprawling and inefficient. Even Triumph in those days was no place for flair. With hindsight, it wasn't so much a question of 'Will it collapse', as 'When will it collapse?'

By 1969, the year that Honda's staggeringly successful CB750-4 went on sale (they sold a

Above: BSA Fury version of the dohc 350cc Bandit.

million), the basic Triumph twin design was 32 years old. Great as it had been, in the year that man first walked on the Moon, it was obsolete. Ironically, the BSA Group had bought a CB750 for evaluation; when its final drive chain snapped and wrecked the engine after less than 160 kilometres (100 miles), they dismissed it. After all, 'everyone knew the Japanese couldn't make big bikes.'

Nowhere was the impact of Japanese bikes greater than in the USA. Successful as the British had been there, they did little to turn on the mass of Americans to two wheels. In the mid-Fifties the US market amounted to around 50,000 machines per year. By 1971, after the Oriental invasion, it stood at

2.1 *million*. The Japanese didn't steal the motorcycle mass market: they invented it. They did so with exciting, technically advanced machinery at an affordable price. Sound familiar? That's exactly what Triumph did to Harley in 1951.

In truth, BSA/Triumph did have many exciting prototypes in the post-war years, including a 700cc ohv straight four as early as 1949, and an overhead camshaft 500cc twin in 1952. In 1967 Turner himself was brought out of retirement to design a 34bhp, dohc 350cc twin capable of 180km/h (112mph). This, the BSA Fury-Triumph Bandit project, was brought to the verge of fruition by Doug Hele and Bert Hopwood. Although shown

to the press in November 1970, it never quite reached production. Even the Trident, the sole worthwhile model to reach the showrooms, was a stop-gap measure: too little, and too late.

It's one thing to underestimate your rivals, quite another to regard the public in the same light. For the plain fact was that the British motorcycle industry was at best growing deaf to customer aspirations. At worst, they were treated with with increasing contempt, an attitude which could do nothing for sales. Sadly, it was to take a painful collapse and rebirth before this lesson was learned.

Triumph Trident 750

THE TRIDENT 750 and its BSA stablemate, the Rocket-3, signalled Triumph's entry into the new world of street-going 'superbikes'. The triple was in some ways a better machine than Honda's shattering CB750 launched one year later. It was at least as fast and certainly handled far better. Yet somehow it was a half-measure which never quite cut it against the sophistication and sheer flamboyance of the four.

Originally the BSA Group produced two versions, the Triumph Trident T150 and the BSA

Below: Arguably the first true superbike, the Trident could not quite match the refinement of Honda's slightly later CB750-four.

Rocket-3. The latter used forward-inclined cylinders in a tubular twin cradle, compared to the Triumph's upright powerplant in a single-downtube 650-type frame.

Essentially, this was one-and-a-half Triumph Daytonas on a common crankcase, a stop-gap measure initiated by two of the rare forward-thinkers in the British industry at the time, Bert Hopwood and Doug Hele. Indeed Hopwood had also proposed a far more advanced and comprehensive family of 'modular' engines not unlike that adopted by the Bloor/Triumph company 20 years later. Although a far less sophisticated design than Honda's overhead cam-four, it produced strong power from a relatively

SPECIFICATION	TRIDENT T150
ENGINE	740cc ohv tranverse triple
POWER	58bhp @ 7500rpm
TRANSMISSION	5-speed
WHEELBASE	1473mm (58in)
WEIGHT	209kg (460lb)
TOP SPEED	193km/h (120mph)

smooth-running package and just might have supported Triumph until more modern engines could come on-stream.

In the meantime, the Trident would have to suffice against the Japanese multis, and it did so pretty well. A good one was at least as fast as the Honda – the first press-test Trident, possibly a 'special', clocked almost 209km/h (130mph); others struggled to reach 190km/h (118mph). The handling, though good, was undoubtedly compromised by the sheer mass of the beast. Nonetheless, it could leave the Honda for dead through the turns.

Mechanically, though, this was the triple that Edward Turner might have designed in 1937. Push-rods opened the valves, at a time when overhead camshafts were becoming commonplace. The crankcases split vertically, like the twin's, and primary drive was by chain. A diaphragm clutch was more up-to-date, but the original four-speed gearbox was not. Overall, despite Ogle Design's styling (with 'Ray-gun' silencers and 'Bread-bin' fuel tank), the bike was more a child of the Sixties than the imminent Seventies.

Right: Trident styling was by Ogle Design, although this 1974 T150V example lacks the original 'ray-gun' silencers.

55

Where the triple scored its biggest success was on the track, where anyone who heard it still shivers from that haunting wail. For British race fans of the seventies, the Rob North-framed triple was the 'feel-good' factor on two wheels: first, second and third at Daytona in 1971; countless other short-circuit victories; and a succession of production TT wins for the legendary 'Slippery Sam'.

On early versions the equipment, too, was sometimes inadequate. Triumph's twin leading-shoe drum front brake was never very potent; on the 209kg (460lb) triple it was downright embarrassing. Starting, unlike the Honda's, was by kick. Despite a higher selling price (£747 in 1973), it simply wasn't as refined as the Honda.

When it finally arrived, the Triumph-Lockheed disc front brake was good, but by then the triple had been five years in production. Also in

Left and above: 1975 marked the arrival of the ultimate Trident, the T160, now with electric start, disc brakes and forward-slanting cylinders like the BSA Rocket-3. Triumph lacked sufficient faith in the Prestolite starters – originally purchased for an abortive electric-start Norton Commando – to ditch the kick start. Right: Craig Vetter's X-75 Hurricane was a bold attempt to woo American buyers.

1973, attempts to improve sales resulted in the X-75 Hurricane, one of the most eye-catching roadsters ever produced: it flopped. Two years later still the Triumph T160 electric-start version appeared, now with more power from an engine leaning forward in the old Rocket-3 manner. Sadly it was all too little, and too late.

Co-operation and Collapse

ALTHOUGH THEY had joined forces in 1951, it wasn't until 1968 that Triumph and BSA fully collaborated on production models, notably on the new Trident and Rocket-3 range of 741cc triples. Despite the considerable detail differences between them, all triple engines were actually built at BSA's Small Heath plant, with frame fabrication and final assembly at Meriden. Other joint efforts were a new type of oil-bearing spine frame, common to the BSA and Triumph big twins; and a new 250cc 'Triumph', the TR25W Trailblazer, that was actually a re-badged BSA 250SS.

In late '72 the first 750cc Bonneville appeared, but it brought no salvation. Within months the BSA Group was bankrupt. Worse still, when a hasty rescue package was announced in September 1973, it threatened to consign Triumph to history. The proposals were that Dennis Poore's Norton-Villiers would take over BSA's motorcycle operations. Meriden would be closed, with production switched to Small Heath. The Triumph name looked likely to be dropped altogether, or switched to cheaper Norton models. Worst of all, at least 1500 redundancies were expected.

It was too much. Meriden's workers occupied their factory. Management was locked out, 2500 finished machines were locked in. Worse still for the parent company, Trident production ground to a halt for several months before it could be resumed at Small Heath.

Above: The Silver Jubilee Bonneville marked 25 years on the throne for Elizabeth, and 40 years of Edward Turner's Triumph twin. Left: A 1978 T140 Bonneville, now 750cc and Coop-built, but the same classic lines. Right: Final Bonnevilles featured cast wheels.

Then, in February 1974, a new Labour government was elected with far more sympathy for Meriden's plight than the out-going Conservatives had shown. On 10 July 1974 industry minister Tony Benn announced the creation of the Meriden Motorcycle Co-operative, aided by a £5 million grant. The deal included an unwieldy compromise in which the Co-op would build TR7V Tiger and Bonneville twins, but Norton-Villiers, who retained the Triumph name and rights, would control sales and marketing. Somewhat incidentally, the triples disappeared.

By the time actual production began in March 1975 no Triumph twins had been built for two years, to the detriment of dealers and markets. A lifesaving deal was reached in which the giant GEC company bought 2000 Bonnies, providing £1 million of ready capital. GEC also advised on establishing a sales and marketing operation, and in 1977 Meriden finally acquired the full rights to its products. To celebrate, they introduced the limited edition Jubilee Special model, for this was also the Queen's 25th year as reigning monarch.

What Meriden really needed, however, was an entirely new engine, a fact which the Jubilee and other cosmetic exercises could not disguise. America

was still by far their largest market, taking 60 per cent of up to 350 machines per week produced. But even here emissions regulations were threatening to outlaw the elderly twin. A replacement was promised – the 'Diana', a liquid-cooled, balance shafted 900cc twin – but progress was desperately slow in the under-capitalized company.

In 1983 the Co-op finally collapsed and by mid-1984 Meriden was no more than a pile of rubble. Although Labour's 'bold experiment' is now regarded as a failure, it did secure the Triumph name

for a further eight years – and, not least, the livelihoods of hundreds of men and women.

But even now the grand old name refused to die. In the short-term, small-scale production switched to, of all places, Newton Abbot, Devon. Here, Les Williams' tiny company built up to 14 new twins per week under licence, as well as providing spares for thousands already on the road.

As to the longer term, a little-known Midlands builder named John Bloor bought the Triumph name . . .

Rebirth: Bloor Triumph

Below: Hinckley's 900 triple, here housed in an Adventurer, has emerged as one of the great engines of the Nineties: characterful, unbreakable and lusty.

JOHN BLOOR did more than simply redesign Triumph's logo. In September 1990, when the motorcycle press were first allowed beyond Triumph's tight security, they were staggered by what they saw. For almost a decade this grand old marque had been all-but written off. But now a brand-new 8360m² (90,000 square feet) factory on the outskirts of Hinckley, Leicestershire, was packed with the best computerized machine tools money could buy. No motorcycle plant on earth was more modern.

The pre-production models on display that day were just as remarkable: two triples, a 750cc roadster and a 900cc sports tourer. But just as impressive was the attitude of the born-again company. Gone was the old take-it-or-leave it approach. Missing was the presumption that because they had a grand old name, they had a great new product. In fact it was to be more than a year before the factory proclaimed itself 'Triumph' at all.

One man made this miracle happen. John Bloor, a former plasterer, became a millionaire many times over building houses in the north Midlands. For reasons which are not entirely clear, the enigmatic 53-year-old decided to sink a substantial portion of his personal fortune into re-inventing Triumph, the rights to which he had bought in 1983.

When work began at Bloor Holdings' headquarters in Measham, it was hoped that the Diana engine begun at Meriden could form the

Above: Early left-side plumbing has been cleaned up.

The versatile triple powers machines as diverse as Sprint (above), Speed Triple (below), not to mention Trident, Tiger, T'bird, Adventurer, Trophy and Daytona.

61

basis of a new model range. However, it soon became clear that the liquid-cooled twin could not deliver the performance or characteristics required. Eventually a modular approach was arrived at, offering three- and four-cylinder variants ranging from 750 to 1200cc. By adopting this approach, Triumph could save appreciably on tooling, manufacturing costs and R&D. The engines themselves were massively over-engineered, partly to overcome the old reputation for oil leaks and breakdowns. As early as 1985, the spine frame common to every model was chosen because it offered a wide variety of styling options and was cheap to produce.

Even so, ventures like this do not happen overnight, or come cheap. With the demise of the Diana engine, seven years were to elapse before a complete new prototype was assembled for testing. Bloor Holdings' accounts for 1991 recorded a fall in pre-tax profits, from £21.5 million to £8.7 million. Most of the shortfall was eaten by the voracious new baby at Hinckley. To date, something like £90 million has been sunk into the factory and its plant. It is inconceivable that this could have happened had Bloor needed to raise share or venture capital, rather than unfolding it from his own hip pocket.

The other thing Bloor has undoubtedly raised is morale – both of his own workforce, and of the British motorcycle fraternity in general. A cornerstone of the new range was the undertaking of a thorough evaluation of competing models (mainly Japanese), and of the methods which produced them. For the first time in British motorcycle production history, design and manufacture were closely linked – not only by a factory's technology but by its people. And above all, 'New Triumph' listened to its customers. It was about time.

Into the Nineties

Below: Hinckley Trident takes its ease on a New Zealand beach. Although not the fastest machine in its class, the Trident's sure handling and easy power are a tourer's delight.

BLOOR-Triumph's first model range, unveiled in the autumn of 1990 in Cologne, comprised six models. The unfaired Trident was available with 750 or 900cc three-cylinder engines; the Trophy tourers came as a 900cc three or a 1200cc four; and the sporting Daytonas both harnessed short-stroke engines of either 750 or 1000cc.

Despite some buyer caution, the new range went down well, both at the shows and in the shops. 2390 machines were sold, of which 974 went into UK showrooms, broken down as follows: 1200 Trophy, 334; 900 Trophy, 136; 1000 Daytona, 165; 750 Daytona, 68; 900 Trident, 196; 750 Trident, 75.

But it was equally clear that the range lacked differentiation and – other than the brilliant Tridents – a solid identity. Customers also didn't see why the most sporting model, the big Daytona, couldn't have the strongest engine, the 1200 four. Since then Hinckley has listened to its markets, steadily learned its lessons, the range becoming more focussed each year. Along the way the 1000 four disappeared altogether, whilst the short-stroke 750 has been confined to the 'entry level' Trident. By 1996 the universally-acclaimed 900cc triple is the lynchpin of the Hinckley range, powering nine of the 12-bike fleet and accounting for 80 to 90 per cent of sales.

Manufacturing, too, has made meteoric progress. When Triumph first launched their 1991 model range, they were struggling to make eight bikes per day. Now they comfortably average 60 – 15,000

MODULAR MAGIC

The Hinckley line-up is based on a modular approach broadly similar to that proposed by Bert Hopwood in the Seventies. This highly cost-effective philosophy utilizes two basic cylinder types: the short-stroke engine (76 x 55mm) displaces 250cc per pot, whilst the long-stroke shares the same bore but with a 65mm stroke to give 295cc. Multiplying this by three or four gives all four engine types. Fittingly, one of the specialist companies consulting on these developments was the same Ricardo Engineering whose founder had created the four-valve Ricardo Triumph in 1921.

Other main specifications are identical: across-the-frame, liquid-cooled, double overhead camshafts, four valves and one carb per cylinder. Transmissions are mainly six-speed, with the Speed Triple, Adventurer and Thunderbird having one ratio fewer.

Modifications to compression ratio and ignition and valve timing also offer four distinct states of tune. Prior to the new superbikes in the 1997 range, the Super-3 and 1200 Daytona offered the highest specific output, the hugely tractable Thunderbird and Adventurer the least.

units per year – with their sights set far higher when an even larger additional factory comes on stream.

There were initial problems – with head gaskets, flooding carbs, plug caps, and the Daytona's camchain tensioner – but most were minor and all were quickly fixed. Once chiefly associated with vibration and oil leaks, Triumph is now a by-word for solid engineering and high-quality finish.

As well as a 21st century factory, Triumph have marketed their wares abroad with a vigour not seen since the Fifties. By late 1993 Triumphs were on sale in Germany, Italy, France, Belgium, Holland, New Zealand, Japan, Australia, Spain, Switzerland, Portugal, Greece and Argentina. A year later Canada

Below: The stunning 1997 T509 uses aluminium T595 chassis to update the successful Speed Triple concept.

Right: New for '97, the gloriously styled T595 grew from the 900 Daytona concept, but is a lighter, smaller, faster package: a real rival for Ducati's 916.

63

followed, and then in 1995 it was back to the big one: the USA. By then the project which began as an obscure Midlands joke was well on the way to becoming a global triumph.

For 1997 even more exciting models are poised, headed by the T509 superbike, prototypes of which have already been seen in action. This will benefit from an all-new lightweight beam frame, even more power and state-of-the-art fuel injection currently developed by an Anglo-French company.

Triumph Daytona 900 and 1200

ALTHOUGH THE 1991 Daytonas housed short-stroke engines (90bhp 750 three and 121bhp 1000 four), by 1993 the range had assumed much of its present form, comprising a 900cc triple and 1200 four. The Daytonas are Hinckley's most sporting models, boasting the best suspension components and brakes, and with the most racy styling and riding positions. The triple produces 99bhp, the highly-tuned 1200 a staggering 147bhp, both at 9500rpm.

Despite the connotations of the name, Daytonas are the sports tourers of the Triumph range, much more ZZ-R1100 than CBR900. Street racers will find them heavy and tall, but for demolishing long distances they have few equals. With both versions, strong, flexible engines combine with unimpeachable stability and superb high-speed steering to give effortless high-speed performance.

Brakes and suspension are – the Super III's six-piston calipers excepted – the best in the Hinckley range. The 900, of course, boasts that irresistible three-cylinder engine, and feels a better balanced overall package than the four. The 1200, despite a claimed 147PS, can't quite match the ZZ-R1100 for performance – although, at over 257km/h (160mph), it is ridiculously fast.

Like all modern Triumphs, finish – and particularly corrosion resistance – is superb (one of the benefits of it being developed in a salt-encrusted country). And very few other engines are this bullet-proof.

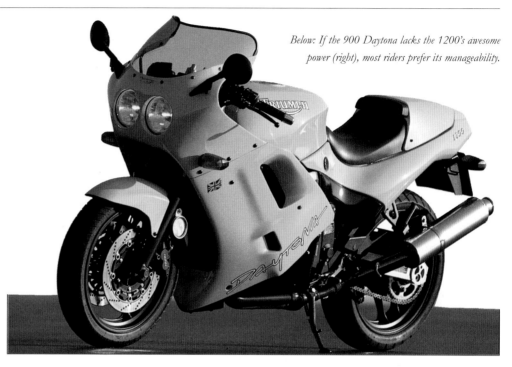

Below: If the 900 Daytona lacks the 1200's awesome power (right), most riders prefer its manageability.

SPECIFICATION	DAYTONA 900
ENGINE	885cc 4-stroke, 3-cyl, dohc water-cooled
POWER	98bhp @ 9000rpm
TRANSMISSION	6-speed
TORQUE	61lb.ft @ 6500rpm
WHEELBASE	1490mm (58.7in)
FUEL TANK	25 litres (5.5 gallons)
WEIGHT	233kg (514lb) (with full tank)
TOP SPEED	232km/h (144mph)

SPECIFICATION	DAYTONA 1200
ENGINE	1180cc 4-stroke, 4-cyl, dohc water-cooled
POWER	147bhp @ 9500rpm
TRANSMISSION	6-speed
TORQUE	85lb.ft @ 8000rpm
WHEELBASE	1490mm (58.7in)
FUEL TANK	25 litres (5.5 gallons)
WEIGHT	245kg (540lb) (with full tank)
TOP SPEED	259km/h (161mph)

Triumph Daytona Super III

INTRODUCED in 1994, the limited edition Super III was Triumph's misconceived attempt to compete with Japanese super-sports machines. The Super III features a lightened (by Cosworth) and tuned version of the usual triple engine, in substantially the same tune as the 1200 Daytona. Unfortunately the attempt fails because the tall, heavy engine and lofty spine frame preclude any current Triumph from behaving like Suzuki's slimline GSX-R. In practice, what you get instead is a slightly less flexible Daytona with added carbon fibre at an inflated price (£10,294 in 1996, £500 more than a Daytona 1200). The British-made six-piston brakes, though, are absolutely superb.

Above and left: Possibly Hinckley's biggest mistake: the Super III offered little the Daytona could not provide, but cost a great deal more. The six piston brakes, though, are absolutely superb at any speed.

SPECIFICATION	DAYTONA SUPER III
ENGINE	885cc 4-stroke, 3-cyl, dohc water-cooled
POWER	115bhp @ 9500rpm
TRANSMISSION	6-speed
TORQUE	66lb.ft @ 8500rpm
WHEELBASE	1490mm (58.7in)
FUEL TANK	25 litres (5.5 gallons)
WEIGHT	231kg (509lb) (with full tank)
TOP SPEED	238km/h (148mph)

Triumph Trophy 900 and 1200

ALTHOUGH THE name first arose from Triumph's off road exploits, the Trophies are the sports-tourers of the Hinckley range, designed to gobble up huge mileages with minimal effort. Like all Triumphs, their strengths are a bullish, bullet-proof engine and solid if slightly ponderous handling. Like the rest of the range, both the 900 and 1200cc engines use balance shafts for vibe-free running. The 1200 is one of the smoothest, strongest fours in motorcycling, if slightly anodyne compared with the characterful triple, which is identical to the Daytona powerplant. The only major shortcoming of early examples – inadequate brakes – was solved with the adoption of Daytona four-pot calipers in 1994.

Early Trophies were slightly lacking in long-haul comfort, but were progressively improved by modifications to seat, screen and riding position.

For 1993 the 1200's peak power was reduced from 125 to 108bhp in the interests of enhancing its already prodigious torque, with a further 2bhp reduction in '96. Peak torque – and instant acceleration – now arrives at a relaxed 5000rpm.

1996 also brought the Trophy's first comprehensive redesign, with all-new bodywork, better instruments and more expansive seat and riding position. The fairing was wind-tunnel tested to reduce rider and passenger fatigue, and the overall quality has been favourably compared to

Below: Trophies used to be off-road machines. This, unmistakably, is a grand tourer.

Honda's VFR750 – high praise, indeed. If early versions suffered from being too similar to the sporting Daytonas, they now rank amongst the finest grand tourers in motorcycling. A comprehensive range of integrated custom extras is available to make them even more the superlative high-speed gentleman's carriage.

SPECIFICATION	TROPHY 900
ENGINE	885cc 4-stroke, 3-cyl, dohc water-cooled
POWER	98bhp @ 9000rpm
TRANSMISSION	6-speed
TORQUE	61lb.ft @ 6500rpm
WHEELBASE	1490mm (58.7in)
FUEL TANK	25 litres (5.5 gallons)
WEIGHT	237kg (522lb) (with full tank)
TOP SPEED	228km/h (142mph)

SPECIFICATION	TROPHY 1200
ENGINE	1180cc 4-stroke, 4-cyl, dohc water-cooled
POWER	108bhp @ 9000rpm
TRANSMISSION	6-speed
TORQUE	77lb.ft @ 5000rpm
WHEELBASE	1490mm (58.7in)
FUEL TANK	25 litres (5.5 gallons)
WEIGHT	275kg (606lb) (with full tank)
TOP SPEED	248km/h (154mph)

67

Triumph Sprint 900

Below: The totally usable Triumph. 900 Sprint is Hinckley's most versatile model: not too flash but hugely tractable and comfortable, one- or two-up.

IF THE 900 Trident has become the definitive Triumph, and the Speed Triple the most fun, then the Sprint has to be the most versatile. The half-fairing allows the effortless power of the Trident to be used to the full, resulting in a machine deceptively easy to ride fast. Ironically the concept was not really Hinckley's but a response to several aftermarket suppliers who had garbed the Trident in similar guise.

Although visually a half-faired Trident, with which it shares frame and engine, the Sprint has always had more in common with the Daytona, from which it inherited the suspension and brakes. For 1995, it acquired the 17in rear wheel and

68

Above: It can scratch, too.

SPECIFICATION	SPRINT 900
ENGINE	885cc 4-stroke, 3-cyl, dohc water-cooled
POWER	98bhp @ 9000rpm
TRANSMISSION	6-speed
TORQUE	61lb.ft @ 6500rpm
WHEELBASE	1490mm (58.7in)
FUEL TANK	25 litres (5.5 gallons)
WEIGHT	235kg (518lb) (with full tank)
TOP SPEED	219km/h (136mph)

170/60 tyre grafted on to the Daytonas a year earlier, along with more attractive revised rear bodywork (now also found on the '96 Trophy). The result is a superbly practical machine, worthy winner of the title 'best roadster' awarded in 1995 by the prestigious American magazine, *Cycle World*. A classic, which will surely run and run.

Below: The Sprint concept arose when aftermarket suppliers grafted half-fairings onto Tridents. Within a year Triumph had got in on the act – and with a better chassis, too.

69

Triumph Speed Triple

IF THE Super III was the biggest let-down of the '94 range, the Speed Triple was the success. More than any other Triumph, this one had presence and charisma – not quite like Ducati's sensational M900 Monster, but close: the meanest, moodiest triple since Laverda's Jota ruled the roads

Above: Not all Speed Triples are black, except in spirit. This is the coolest, meanest model in the Hinckley range.

Above: The Speed Triple engine has five speeds, one less than most other 900s. The power spread is so huge, nobody needs the missing ratio.

70

Mechanically, this is a Trident 900 with superior suspension and an engine limited to five gears but otherwise identical. Such is the flexibility of the triple, that no-one missed the extra ratio. The biggest difference is low handlebars and slightly rear-set footpegs, which transform the feel of the machine: more focused through turns, less stressful at speed.

Although also available in vibrant orange, the Triple's true colour is mean black: an urban guerrilla, but equally at home sparking footpegs on country backroads. This is the ultimate style statement in the new Triumph range. And not the least of its strengths is that it achieves all this without compromising function: great brakes, good handling and Triumph's special brand of strong easy power. It is, in short, simply a great motorcycle.

SPECIFICATION	SPEED TRIPLE
ENGINE	885cc 4-stroke, 3-cyl, dohc water-cooled
POWER	98bhp @ 9000rpm
TRANSMISSION	5-speed
TORQUE	61lb.ft @ 6500rpm
WHEELBASE	1490mm (58.7in)
FUEL TANK	25 litres (5.5 gallons)
WEIGHT	229kg (505lb) (with full tank)
TOP SPEED	217km/h (135mph)

Left and below: 'Urban Guerrilla' Speed Triple styling makes the most of the Triumph's naturally beefy lines. Prior to the new T595/T509, this was possibly the model best received by magazine road tests.

Triumph Trident

ESSENTIALLY unchanged since 1994, and visually little different from '91, the two unfaired Trident triples are the staple fare of the Triumph range. Most other manufacturers would have dubbed them 'retros', but to Triumph they are simply motorcycles: straightforward, honest and businesslike, extremely well finished, but with more character than most of the competition.

The 'entry-level' 750 uses the only remaining short-stroke motor from the original Triumph line-up. The 76 x 55mm engine is the revver of the range, and seems to suit the 'little' Trident best. The chassis is less compelling than the powerplant but works well enough and – like all Triumph roadsters – offers superb high speed stability and steering.

The Trident 900, meanwhile, has become the seminal modern Triumph: a practical machine which proves that unfaired bikes don't have to be bland. The secret lies in the engine which, whilst not so addictive as a big Ducati, manages to combine manners and madness like few others. Only long-stroke triples seem to offer quite this effortless blend of bottomless mid-range and manic revability.

Below: No 'retro' machine, but the very first Hinckley Trident was biking at its most uncluttered – and best?

Above: Pinstriping harks back to former days.

SPECIFICATION	TRIDENT 750
ENGINE	749cc 4-stroke, 3-cyl, dohc water-cooled
POWER	90bhp @ 10,000rpm
TRANSMISSION	6-speed
TORQUE	50lb.ft @ 8700rpm
WHEELBASE	1510mm (59.5in)
FUEL TANK	25 litres (5.5 gallons)
WEIGHT	232kg (511lb) (with full tank)
TOP SPEED	212km/h (132mph)

SPECIFICATION	TRIDENT 900
ENGINE	885cc 4-stroke, 3-cyl, dohc water-cooled
POWER	98bhp @ 9000rpm
TRANSMISSION	6-speed
TORQUE	61lb.ft @ 6500rpm
WHEELBASE	1510mm (59.5in)
FUEL TANK	25 litres (5.5 gallons)
WEIGHT	232kg (511lb) (with full tank)
TOP SPEED	217km/h (135mph)

Triumph Tiger 900

D ESPITE ITS name, the Tiger 'super trailie' is more of a descendant of the Trophies of Triumph's past. The off-road pretensions, however, are pure window-dressing. This is far more of a boulevard cruiser in the French style, than any sort of serious desert machine. More than any Hinckley Triumph before it, the big Tiger was created by its market – in this case the continental passion for Paris-Dakar style roadsters. It has sold well in Europe, less so at home, largely because the fastest always seems to sell, and the Tiger is the fastest,

most brutish monster trailie on the market. If nothing else, it gets you noticed.

The already strong Trident 900-based engine is tuned for yet more bottom-end, at the price of less willingness to rev at the top. The Tiger is the strongest, heaviest, most be-cylindered 'dirt bike' on the market, a machine only a madman would take off-road. On the other hand it does make a surprisingly competent tourer, ready to demolish huge mileages with the ability also to tackle a little gentle exploration at journey's end.

SPECIFICATION	TIGER 900
ENGINE	885cc 4-stroke, 3-cyl, dohc water-cooled
POWER	85bhp @ 8000rpm
TRANSMISSION	6-speed
TORQUE	61lb.ft @ 6000rpm
WHEELBASE	1560mm (61in)
FUEL TANK	24 litres (5.3 gallons)
WEIGHT	228kg (503lb) (with full tank)
TOP SPEED	209km/h (130mph)

Below left and below: The massive Tiger could maul you on dirt – it's not really a trail bike at all, but an imposing long-haul cruiser.

73

The New Look

TRIUMPH sprang a big surprise with the launch of their 900 Thunderbird in the autumn of 1994. The evocative name, of course, was inherited from the 650cc twin which had spearheaded Triumph's drive into the US market in the early Fifties. This was no coincidence, for the new T'bird was designed for precisely the same role.

This was a major departure for Hinckley. Although based on the same frame and three-cylinder engine as existing models, the concept was entirely new, for form now dominated function.

The T'bird was strictly neither retro nor custom, yet intended to evoke a sense of free-wheeling style which would appeal to American buyers. Functionally, it is the least able of all Triumph's models, with inferior handling, brakes and power. And yet it instantly struck a ready chord. Hinckley's production plans had to be rapidly revised to cope with the massive demand.

From its old-style 'harmonica' tank badge to its classic seat and 16in rear wheel, the T'bird is the first new model expressly designed to play on Triumph's nostalgia quotient. Mechanically, it is much like any other naked Triumph triple: spine frame, similar front and rear suspension to the Trident (albeit without rebound damping), but with the longest wheelbase amongst the roadster range. 'Classic' wire wheels are used. The familiar, but cosmetically re-styled, three-cylinder engine employs the same five speeds as the Speed Triple. Power is substantially less than other versions at 70bhp, although peak torque arrives much earlier than even the Tiger's at 4800rpm.

A year later the Adventurer caused a bigger stir still. Essentially an even more stylized Thunderbird (and £190 dearer), this goes to new extremes on the chrome and tassels department, the nearest Triumph has come to a true custom model. Its detractors have dismissed it as an unworthy victory of style over substance, for the tall three-cylinder engine scarcely lends itself to Harley-type lowrider looks. However, it will be to their order books that Triumph will look for justification, and the early signs are that the newcomer will be a considerable export success.

Both models are accompanied by a stylish new range of custom and riding goodies, designed and manufactured for Triumph to complement their new models. This is an area pioneered so profitably by Harley-Davidson, whose customer loyalty (and spending power) is the envy of every other manufacturer. 'Triumph modes' have yet to make the Paris catwalks, but they could become a major weapon in Triumph's return to form.

Left: Panniers, screen and other bolt-on goodies signal Triumph's move into profitable aftermarket wares.

SPECIFICATION	THUNDERBIRD
ENGINE	885cc 4-stroke, 3-cyl, dohc water-cooled
POWER	70bhp @ 8000rpm
TRANSMISSION	5-speed
TORQUE	53lb.ft @ 4800rpm
WHEELBASE	1550mm (61in)
FUEL TANK	15 litres (3.3 gallons)
WEIGHT	234kg (516lb) (with full tank) (Adventurer 237kg/522lb)
TOP SPEED	196km/h (122mph)

Left: The Adventurer attempts to emulate Harley cruiser style. For many, the experiment does not work: too short, too tall, too much chrome and too little good taste.

Left and above: The Thunderbird is a more stylish attempt at something different, and has rapidly become Triumph's best seller.

75

The Dream Factory

FOR ANYONE who has seen the inside of a British motorcycle factory, the treasures revealed on a visit to Dodwells Bridge Industrial Estate are almost too staggering to comprehend. Occupying some 8,360m² (90,000 square feet) on a 4-hectare (10-acre) green field site, the new plant is bright, clean and air-conditioned. But anyone addicted to the sounds and smells of heavy engineering and cutting oils is likely to be disappointed. The noise of manufacturing is more of a distant high-tech hum, the atmosphere calm and controlled.

The machinery on show is the very latest in automated, computer-controlled design. This not only keeps labour costs low – each employee makes an average of around 40 machines per year – but ensures a level of manufacturing accuracy quite unknown to Meriden's workers, to whom the new facility would seem like a stage set from *Star Wars*.

But Triumph is about more than hardware. Mass-producing complex modern motorcycles is a process of mind-boggling complexity in which the contribution of people is as crucial as that of machines. So the ethos of the new factory is equally

Above: Hinckley's final assembly line pours out new machines in ever-increasing numbers. Left: Gleaming 900 Triples en route to an eager market.

dedicated to precision and quality. Not unexpectedly, many of the operational practices adopted at Hinckley originate from Japan. Sometimes directly: Alan Hurd, Hinckley's production engineering manager, recalls that Japanese motorcycle manufacturers, notably Kawasaki, offered considerable practical help in the early days by introducing Triumph staff to their methods and suppliers.

On other occasions the lessons were bought in. John Burton, an early head of production at Hinckley, had run Nissan's huge Washington car body shop before joining Triumph. He set about developing 'the Triumph Way', based on Nissan's

Anglo-Japanese style: 'It's given the staff a bit of a culture shock. When I arrived, there wasn't enough communication. We've opened that up. We get feedback, not only "How many have we made?", but "How well did we make them?" To anyone familiar with old Small Heath ways, this is a refreshing taste of ultra-modern manufacturing.

In 1984, just 14 staff worked for the company at John Bloor's offices in Measham. By the time the first motorcycles rolled off the production line in 1991, the payroll stood at 120. It now stands near 400, with double shift working the norm.

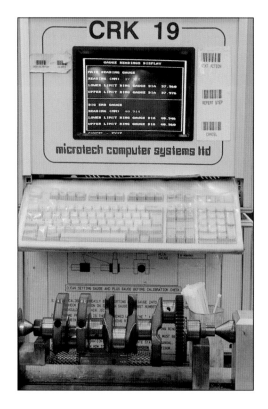

Left: Computerized precision measuring ensures correct crankshaft clearances. Right: High-tech robots weld Triumph frames. Above: But it still takes people to put it all together.

True, there has been some criticism that Hinckley sources too many of its components from overseas. But there was really very little choice, there being almost nothing left of the welter of parts manufacturers which had once supplied the British motorcycle industry. So, much of each modern Triumph motorcycle is imported, mainly from Japan. But a great deal is also built or finished at Hinckley. Indeed, in order to ensure supplies and quality, more work is done in-house than at any other comparable motorcycle facility. On-site processing includes metal treatments such as crank nitriding; the paint shop; final machining of most engine components, from entire crankcases to cam retainers; frame and swing-arm fabrication and finishing; and, of course, painstaking final assembly.

As a production facility, Hinckley is undoubtedly a soaring success. By mid-1996, Triumph had built over 40,000 new machines, with production currently running at around 15,000 units per year. But this counts for nothing if sales are not equally buoyant which, happily, they have been. Every year since 1991, orders have exceeded production. In the UK, Triumph stands second only to Honda in sales of over-750cc machines. Nor does the story end there: as you read this, a bigger, even more modern factory is under construction next door. Triumph plans to enter the 21st century with capacity quadrupled to 60,000 machines per year.

Competition

TRIUMPH'S competition credentials began early – in 1907. That year, of course, is best remembered for the first running of the Isle of Man motorcycle TT (the cars had one in 1906). Although Matchless won the single-cylinder class, Jack Marshall's Triumph finished a worthy second. A year later he went one better, winning at an average speed of 65km/h (40.40mph). However, once their reputation was established, Triumph became much less competition-minded, often preferring to garner publicity through well-publicized endurance tests, such as the Thunderbird Montlhéry marathon,

rather than the uncertain world of racing – for Triumph made 'real world' motorcycles, not mere playthings for racers. It would be another 59 years before they chalked up their second TT success.

So the factory's involvement in road racing was infrequent, and usually due to the enthusiasm of a few individuals. One of these, Ernie Lyons, roared

Below: In 1967 the great Garry Nixon became the first Triumph rider to wear the coveted US #1 plate by winning the AMA championship. He's seen here winning at Daytona in the opening round of the series.

to victory in the 1946 Manx Grand Prix on a special Tiger 100 equipped with a lightweight AAPP top-end. This same construction was later applied to the legendary Grand Prix production racer.

One form of competition to which the factory was more attuned was the gruelling, off-road International Six Day Trial (ISDT). In 1948 Triumph were the only British manufacturers to gain a Team Prize, using special machines which would later lead to the TR5 Trophy model. It was the usual case of using experience directly to improve the breed, and in this case the resulting production machine was rather better than the competition prototype.

Although the Grand Prix twin achieved considerable clubman's success, the arrival of the Bonneville in 1959 truly made Triumph a force to be reckoned with. The 650cc twin, especially in highly-tuned 'Thruxton' spec, scored countless victories at all levels, most notably in winning the Thruxton and Bol d'Or endurance events. But arguably the Bonnie's finest hour came in June 1969 when Malcolm Uphill became the first man to lap the notorious Isle of Man TT course at 161km/h (100mph) on a production machine (christening a Dunlop tyre, the TT100, in the process).

Triumph's first major success in the USA was Buddy Elmore's 1966 win in the prestigious Daytona 200-mile road race. But the title that really counts over there is the Number One plate, awarded since 1946 to the top rider through a gruelling series of road race, dirt track and 'TT steeplechase' events. Triumph's first win in the series arrived as early as 1955, but it was to take another dozen years and the arrival of Baltimore's mercurial Gary Nixon before

Triumph stood indisputably at the top of the pile. Nixon began his 1967 campaign with victory at Daytona, backing this up with further road race, mile and short-track successes to score a resounding 508 to 451 point series win over Harley's George Roeder. Nixon retained the Number One plate in '68, and both Gene Romero and Garry Scott went on to take regular dirt-track wins well into the Seventies.

Although Triumph were never again to win Daytona, the arrival of Doug Hele's glorious triples brought a further flurry of road race successes, not only in the USA but in Europe as well. Perhaps more fitting still was the success of the legendary production racer 'Slippery Sam' in taking back-to-back TT wins in 1974 and '75. It wasn't quite like you could buy in the shops, but – ever the Triumph way – close enough.

Above: Buddy Elmore on his way to taking Triumph's first win in the gruelling Daytona 200-mile race in 1966. Below and left: Meanwhile, there has been plenty of Triumph success, on dirt, too.

Index

AAPP 32
Allen, Johnny 32, 40, 50
Alves, Jim 32
Andrews, William 8
Ariel 20, 22, 34

Barcelona 24-hour race, 50
Bettman, Siegfried 8, 12, 20, 25
Bloor, John 58, 60, 62
Bol d'Or endurance race 76
Bonneville salt flats 32
Bosch 12
Brandish, Walter 18
Brando, Marlon 36, 48
Brooklands 18, 22
BSA 34, 58
Burton, John 74

Catt 12
Coventry, blitz 28
Crickets, The 48

Daimler, Gottlieb 8, 25
Dashwood hill climb 10
Daytona 200 mile race 40, 78
Dean, James 48
Degens, Dave 48
'Diana' engine 58, 60
Docker, Sir Bernard 34
Druid forks 18
Dunlop, Joey 42

Elmore, Buddy 40, 78

Fafnir 8

Gaymer, Bert 32
Griffiths, Frank 52

Halford , Major FB 18

Harley-Davidson 32, 72
Hathaway 12
Hele, Doug 42, 50, 54, 56, 78
Hildebrande and Wolfmller 8
Hinckley 60, 63, 74-5
Holbrook, Col. Claude 14
Honda 52, 56
Hopwood, Bert 28, 42, 54, 56, 63
Horsman, Victor 16, 18
Hulbert, Frank 10
Hyde, Norman 48

Isle of Man TT 10, 18, 30, 76
Ixion 10

JAP 8
Japan 16, 32, 52
Jefferies, Allan (& Nick) 32
Johnson, Bill 40

Kawasaki, and Triumph 74

Lucas Magdyno 20
Lyons, Ernie 28, 30, 76

Manx Grand Prix 76
Manx Grand Prix, 1946 28, 76
Marshall 10
Marshall, Jack 76
Matchless 10
McQueen, Steve 48
Meriden 28, 30, 34, 50
Meriden cooperative 50, 58
Minerva 8
Mods & Rockers 46
Montlhery, circuit 30, 76
Much Park Street 8

National Motor Museum 8
Nissan cars 74

Nixon, Gary 40, 78
Norton-Villiers 58
NSD 16

Page, Val 20, 25-26
Parker, Charles 25
plunger rear suspension 34
Poore, Dennis 58
Priory Street works 10, 20

Ricardo, (Sir) Harry 14, 18, 20
Ricardo, model 14, 16, 18-19

Sangster, Jack 20, 25, 28, 34
Schulte, Mauritz 8, 10, 12, 14, 16, 25
Scott, Gary 78
'Slippery Sam' racer 56, 78
Small Heath 58
sprung fork 10
Sprung Hub 30, 36
Super Seven car 16
Suzuki Super Six 42

Thruxton, endurance race 76
trembler coil 10
Triton 48
Triumph Corporation of America 32
Triumph Engineering Co. Ltd., name 20
Turner, Edward 20, 24-26, 28, 32, 34, 52, 54
Turner, Eric 42

Umberslade Hall 52
unit construction, first 34
Uphill, Malcolm 76
USA, motorcycle market 32, 54

Vale, Harry 32
Vincent motorcycles 36

Wild One, The 48
Williams, Les 58

Yamaha 52

Triumph Model Index:
Model H 12
Model P 16
Model W 16
350 Bandit 54
3HW 28
3T De Luxe 30
3TW 28, 30
5/2, 5/5, 5/10 22
650cc 6/1 20
750cc Bonneville 58
900 Sprint 68
Adventurer 32, 72
Bandit (and BSA Fury) 42, 54
Bonneville 46
Bonneville T120 34, 36, 40, 50
Bonneville T140V 50
CN 20
Daytona 40
Daytona 900 & 1200 64
Fury 54
Gloria 20
Grand Prix 28, 32, 76
Jubilee Special 58
LS 14, 20
LW Junior 12
Model 21 34
'Saint' 36
Silver Jubilee' T140V 50
Speed Triple 69
Speed Twin 22, 24, 26, 30, 32, 34, 36

Super III 65
T100A 34
T120R 50
T509 62
T6 Thunderbird 36
Terrier 34
Thruxton Bonneville 50
Thunderbird 30, 34, 40, 72
Tiger 70, 80, 90 24
Tiger 100C 40
Tiger 100 26, 30, 32
Tiger 110 34, 36, 40
Tiger 900 71
Tiger Cub 34, 42
Tigress 45
Tina 45
TR5 Trophy 28, 32, 76
TR6 Trophy 32, 40
TR7 40
TR7V Tiger 58
Trident 58
Trident 750 (& BSA Rocket-3) 56
Trident 750 & 900 68, 70
Trophy 900 & 1200 66
Trophy Trail 32
Type A 12
Type SD 14
Type TT 18
TRW 28
X-75 Hurricane 56
T100R 32
X05/1, X05/5 22